On top of the world today, he's a man who's hit bottom—and made it back:

TIM ALLEN

Winner. Class clown. Stand-up comedian. Promising new talent on his way to the top.

TIM ALLEN

Loser. Small-time drug dealer. Federal prisoner, playing an extended engagement for his fellow inmates at the bottom of the heap.

TIM ALLEN

Champion. Back, and better than ever. Star of the highest-rated TV show, "Home Improvement," the top-grossing film, "The Santa Clause," and the bestselling book, *Don't Stand Too Close to a Naked Man*. He was named the most powerful star on television by *TV Guide*.

TIM ALLEN

—As you've never seen him before! From smalltime stand-up at Comedy Castle to bigtime superstar to the world.

Other Avon Books by
Michael Arkush

RUSH!

TIM ALLEN LAID BARE

UNAUTHORIZED

MICHAEL ARKUSH

AVON BOOKS NEW YORK

TIM ALLEN LAID BARE: UNAUTHORIZED is an original publication of Avon Books. This work has never before appeared in book form.

AVON BOOKS
A division of
The Hearst Corporation
1350 Avenue of the Americas
New York, New York 10019

First Avon Books Printing: October 1995

AVON TRADEMARK REG. U.S. PAT. OFF. AND IN OTHER COUNTRIES, MARCA REGISTRADA, HECHO EN U.S.A.

Printed in the U.S.A.

RA 10 9 8 7 6 5 4 3 2 1

With love to Pauletta, who fills every day with integrity, intelligence, and imagination

Acknowledgments

Many people contributed to make this book possible. First, I owe a lot of thanks to the stable of Detroit comics, who shared stories about their former colleague and made numerous helpful suggestions. I also want to express my appreciation to Tim Allen's ex-classmates from elementary school in Denver and high school in Birmingham, who offered important observations about the young class cutup.

Most of all, though, I am extremely grateful to newspaper reporters Dan Shriner, Dennis Niemiec, and Jim Tobin, who, on more than a few occasions, used their expertise to assist in this project.

Special thanks to my agent, Edward Novak; my editor, Tom Colgan; my friend, Lorenzo Benet; and my daughter, Jade.

1

Tim Allen had a right to be terrified. He was about to perform again in front of his friends and fellow comics at the Comedy Castle in suburban Detroit. He was about to find out if he could put the past behind him.

He had wasted valuable time. For well over a year, while his competitors were honing their stand-up routines by performing at the hottest new comedy clubs across the country, he had taken his act to a federal prison. They were playing in front of crowds. He was playing in front of criminals. They were trying to make it on "The Tonight Show." He was trying to make it to the next morning.

Tim Allen had been a drug dealer. He sold cocaine to an undercover cop, and was punished for it. The bright and clever kid from the right side of the tracks—affluent Birmingham, Michigan—had somehow gone wrong, and now he faced perhaps one last chance to steer himself in the opposite direc-

1

tion. He was rapidly approaching the age of thirty, and he had little to show for it except a prison record and a lost potential.

Some of the Detroit comics, curious about their old friend, made sure to arrive at the club in time.

Just a couple of years earlier, they had been shocked and saddened when Tim suddenly informed them that he would be going out of town for a while on an extended engagement, and wasn't sure when he'd return.

It didn't pay anything, and the benefits weren't much better, but he didn't really have a choice. Some of the other comics had a good reason to fear they might never see him again.

That was all in the past. Tonight, was the future. But there were many questions.

Like a champion prizefighter who had stayed out of the ring too long while his once-formidable skills slowly rusted away, he, too, had to wonder if he still had his punch. Would his material be witty enough? Would his delivery be precise enough? Would his character be endearing enough? Finally, how would he react to handling the pressure of performing again in front of the people who knew him the best?

The crucial moment finally arrived. Terrified or not, Tim Allen could no longer postpone the mystery. He needed to discover the truth, as disconcerting as it might be. He needed to know if he was a comic or a chameleon.

Tim stepped to the stage, seized the microphone, stared at the crowd, and started his act.

His act, and his new life.

If he did panic, it turned out to be premature. Tim was loose and lively, charming and clever. In just a few minutes of comedy, he erased any doubt.

"It was like he had never left," recalled comedian Tony Hayes. "He was a little rusty but he still had that sense of humor. He actually had a better act when he got out of prison. He came right back into the fold."

Tim has been in the fold ever since. In just over a decade, he has skyrocketed from the Toastmasters Club at the Sandstone Federal Correctional Institution in northern Minnesota to the toast of Tinseltown, from the comic who collected a few bucks a night at the Comedy Castle to the television and film megastar who can command a few million.

He has become America's favorite TV dad, the rightful heir to the long-vacant Cosby throne.

He may not be the father who knows best, but he is the father who does his best.

He may not be the most sensitive man of the nineties, but he is the man who learns from his mistakes.

His appeal extends far beyond the small screen. In 1994 he pulled off an unprecedented show business triple play, scoring with the highest-rated television show, "Home Improvement," the top-grossing film, *The Santa Clause*, and the best-selling book, *Don't Stand Too Close to a Naked Man*. About the only thing he didn't do was open on Broadway.

But who is Tim Allen, and how did he go from local loser to national hero? How did he become, as *TV Guide* anointed him earlier this year, the most powerful star on television?

The official version has been circulated countless times in magazines and newspapers:

Tim Allen rose up gradually through the ranks of Detroit's comedy circuit, branching out to headline clubs in the Midwest and Southeast, and eventually breaking through with a popular special on Showtime.

He then took on Los Angeles, caught the attention of Disney's Jeffrey Katzenberg and Michael Eisner, and landed the lead in a new sitcom. The sitcom became an instant smash, and, presto, he became an instant sensation.

Hollywood thrives on these success stories. When they don't exist, it makes them up, and few can ever tell the difference.

In Tim's case, the story is true enough, though it hardly paints a complete portrait.

It doesn't explain the more compelling evolution of the man, of how a small-time drug dealer without any apparent purpose in life managed to dedicate himself to a big-time career in show business. It doesn't explain how he turned prison into the catalyst that drove him to overcome overwhelming odds.

It doesn't explain who Tim Allen is and who he might yet become.

2

First of all, his real name is not Tim Allen. It's Tim Dick, and with a name like that, you damn well better have a good sense of humor.

Timothy Alan Dick was born on June 13, 1953, in Denver, Colorado, arriving in a country confronting Communism on two fronts: in Korea, where, despite efforts by both sides to seek a lasting truce, the fighting was still going on, and in Washington, where Senator Joseph McCarthy was still scouring the city for any Red traitor he could dig up.

Ike was in the White House, and the Rosenbergs were on their way to the electric chair.

The couple had been convicted of conspiring to transmit atomic secrets to the Soviet Union. Thousands around the world campaigned for mercy, but in June of 1953, the Rosenbergs were executed at Sing Sing Prison, becoming the first United States civilians ever put to death for espionage.

Speaking of death, *Dial M for Murder* was

one of the big shows on Broadway, and the plot was a bit unsettling to highly-regarded New York theater critic Walter Kerr.

Kerr had always assumed that men usually had their way with women, on stage, at least, but this drama shattered his illusion. "Time was when a man could twist a woman's wrist with some confidence that she would buckle prettily," Kerr wrote in the *New York Herald Tribune*. "Nowadays he is lucky if he gets his arm back in one piece."

Walter Kerr was showing sympathy for men. Three decades later, Tim Allen would get the same idea.

Childhood would have to come first, which in his case was about as idyllic as it can possibly get. Denver in the America of the fifties was a rapidly emerging Western outpost, with plenty of wide-open territory for little boys to seek adventures and build dreams.

Dad sold insurance, Mom took care of the house. It was a country that doesn't exist any longer except on television reruns.

"Everyone would get married," said childhood friend Rob Southwick, "have kids, and live in the same neighborhood—the perfect world."

For the Dick family, the perfect world revolved around a big house at 359 Marion Street, just a few blocks from the plush Denver Country Club.

Like many in their neighborhood, they lived a middle-class lifestyle, which, back in the early sixties, actually stood for something. You got to keep a good percentage of what you earned. The American Dream was no mirage.

The neighborhood served as the entire universe. Dozens of youngsters, who lived within a few blocks of each other, got together almost every day to play the games of the street—hide and go seek, kick the can, and war. The purpose of war was to kill each other with plastic guns that fired dried-up peas.

When the combatants finally did agree to a cease-fire, they played on the trampoline, turning into amateur contortionists, always pushing each other to invent more difficult acrobatic maneuvers. They jumped for hours and hours, went home for dinner, and hurried back to finish the competition. Darkness was always greeted as a rude intrusion.

The gang kept busy indoors as well, especially at the Dick residence, the neighborhood's unofficial boardinghouse.

"That's where everybody congregated," recalled friend Chris Schilt. "It was a major hub. We'd have sleepovers at the Dicks with eight, ten, fifteen guys. If you didn't have anything to do, you just went to the Dicks' house and knocked, and there were usually people there." Pool and Monopoly battles in the basement became another ritual.

If the action ever got too slow in the neighborhood, Tim and his resourceful companions devised plenty of alternative ways to escape the boredom. They hopped on their bicycles and went out to see the world, which, to youngsters that age, meant any excursions more than a few blocks away.

The fun and games, however, weren't always so innocent away from 359 Marion

Street. Whether throwing firecrackers into nearby Cherry Creek or tossing snowballs at cars and buses or shooting defenseless little animals with BB guns, the young Tim Dick, like so many other boys, loved to flirt with mischief and enjoyed practical jokes.

Like the night that Tim convinced Rollie Bradford there was a burglar in the house.

Rollie quickly retrieved some of his father's guns out of the glass case and prepared to scare off the intruder. Tim wasn't shaken up in the least, which seemed a bit strange to Rollie. Later, he figured out why. "He made it up," said Bradford, "and I fell for it. There was no burglar. Afterwards, I got into a lot of trouble for getting the guns out."

School offered Tim an opportunity for even more trouble. His behavior at times became so horrible that Tim and his good friend, Bobby Click, were forced to abandon any political aspirations before they reached puberty. They had planned to run against each other for class president one fall, "but within about two weeks of getting to school," Click recalled, "we both had too much detention."

As a budding adolescent, Tim was already working on his stand-up routine. He just didn't know it.

He imitated anyone he found unusual or entertaining, often sticking with a new voice or inflection for weeks, though his routine, even back in the early sixties, attracted its share of hecklers. "He taunted you with that monkey noise," recalled Schilt. "It would drive you crazy. We used to beat him up because we hated it so much."

Tim wasn't the most sensitive student in the school. "I can remember that he'd make jokes at other people's expense sometimes," said ex–classmate Kiki Schomp. "There was a side to it that was always a little bit dark, almost like black humor."

Humor, even black humor, was the weapon Tim relied on to survive. Saddled with Dick as his surname opened him up constantly to the cruelest ridicule and teasing from other kids, and he desperately needed a way to fight back. "Up until I was sixteen years old," he told the *Los Angeles Times*, "I'd say, 'Hi, I'm Tim Dick.' And they'd go, 'Ha, ha, penis.' So I was constantly being related to a penis all the time."

Tim figured out that if he could manage to poke fun at his name first, if he could come up with the most clever, self-deprecating one-liners using the word "Dick," perhaps then he could defuse the impact. It was a lesson Tim never forgot.

He picked up his sense of humor from his dad, Gerald Dick, who loved to make people laugh. "He was always the hit of the party," recalled Gerald's sister, Winifred Ingalls. "Whenever Tim says something amusing," she said, "people we grew up with even now comment at different times that, 'Gerry would have liked that joke.' "

Tim also inherited another important life-long passion from his old man. Gerald Dick was absolutely crazy about cars.

"He'd tinker with cars a lot," Tim told *Friends* magazine in 1991. "He'd always put dual exhaust, different manifolds on. He made the family wagon loud and fast."

On many occasions, Gerald Dick escorted the boys and their buddies to the drag races, explaining to them how each vehicle operated.

"I remember one day going out to a house in Denver," Schilt recalled, "to look at a 1932 Ford Phaeton, and Mr. Dick wanted to get that car so bad. They always had really cool cars, always pretty new, always Fords."

One unlucky neighborhood kid, Schilt said, found out one afternoon exactly how much Gerald Dick treasured his sacred automobiles. "He was leaning on their car, and Mr. Dick went up and smacked him a good one because he didn't want him to scratch the paint. It was their brand-new 1960 Ford station wagon. He had just bought it," Schilt said.

Gerald Dick also took the boys to another hangout in town—the Sears store on First Avenue. Tim and his brothers roamed the aisles checking out the latest hardware. You might call it the original Tool Time.

It was a wonderful way to grow up, and it promised to become even better as Tim approached his teenage years.

He had his friends in school, his gang in the neighborhood, his support system at home. Tim Dick had just about everything an eleven-year-old boy could want, and much more.

3

It didn't last long. On November 21, 1964, his perfect world was torn apart by fate, and there would no way to patch it up ever again.

Almost exactly a year earlier, America had lost its president, and its innocence. This time, it was the Dick family who lost everything.

It started out as another typical Saturday. The big event on the afternoon calendar was the football game between the University of Colorado and its in-state rival, the Air Force Academy. Gerald Dick, his wife Martha, two of their sons, and five other boys from the neighborhood squeezed into the station wagon for the short journey to Boulder.

Tim, who went to many of the football games, didn't make the trip. At the last minute, he decided to stay near the house to hang out with Bobby Click. They didn't have a plan, and they didn't need one. "We just played around," recalled Click. "I think maybe we listened to the game on the radio."

The game, for a change, turned out well for the home team. Withstanding the high-powered Air Force passing attack, the Buffaloes won 28-23 thanks to two long punt returns by Ted Somerville and George Lewark.

Afterward, Gerald Dick took the Valley Highway back to Denver. He was cruising along with no problem, when, suddenly, out of nowhere, a car coming from the opposite direction left the highway, struck a speed sign, crossed the median strip, flew into the air, and headed toward the Dicks' station wagon.

Gerald Dick had only a split second to react, and, according to Chris Schilt, who was in the backseat, there was only one thing he could do.

"All of a sudden, I looked up and there was the bottom of a car coming at our car," recalled Schilt. "Gerry swerved and took the entire impact of the car upon himself. It could've been a straight-on. He was an expert driver. I really think he saved my life."

The injuries turned out to be fairly minor: Schilt cut his lip, Tim's brother, David, suffered facial cuts. Martha Dick, Steve Dick, and the other boys were okay. Considering the speed of both vehicles and the impact of the crash, the toll could have been far more severe. Gerald Dick had done his job very well.

But, as usual, heroism called for at least one sacrifice. At forty, Gerald Dick was dead.

It was a horrible blow to his wife and six young children. At Ascension Church the next day, the kids, Ingalls said kept asking, "Why daddy? Why daddy?" Nobody had a good answer.

A drunk driver crashes into an innocent man returning from a football game with his loving family and kids from the neighborhood. The drunk driver walks away without the slightest injury. The innocent man is dead. Nobody would ever have an answer.

The funeral drew a big crowd. Gerald Dick was young and extremely popular. He had been president of the Denver Insurors Association, and was very active in the community. "They overflowed the church," Schilt recalled.

What now? How does a family of five young boys and one girl rebuild their lives after they lose their beloved father? How do they ever restore any semblance of peace again?

The impossible task fell to Martha Dick, the grieving widow. She had always done a magnificent job of keeping a household of young boys from ever going out of control. Now things had definitely gone out of control, and she was the only one who could put things back in order.

A month after the accident, the family spent Christmas in Michigan. Martha had grown up in the area before she attended the University of Colorado and met her future husband, and she still had many close relatives there. She must have known how important it was for the children to be around other family members, to show them that life could go on without their father.

On a later trip back to Michigan, she renewed her friendship with William Bones, an executive with RCA, who had been her high school sweetheart. Bones, unfortunately, could empathize with his former girlfriend. His ex-wife had been critically injured in an automobile accident, which left him in charge of three young children.

Neither, however, was in a big hurry to start a serious relationship. "When you've got six children to take care of," Ingalls said, "you don't have much time for anything else."

Back in Denver, as the months passed, the family tried to resume as many normal activities as possible. Tim was still the same old Tim, making jokes, always hunting for the next adventure.

He hid his pain from everyone around him, but he couldn't hide it from himself. "I never grieved for him properly," Tim told *People* magazine in 1992, "but I constantly thought about him. It's severe emotional baggage, and you never let it go." In his 1994 book, Allen said his father's death made him feel "helpless, useless, pathetic. I had no control, and my scramble to regain some made me grow up very quickly."

The other kids in the neighborhood began to mature, as well, heading off to the intimidating world of junior high school, making new friends, discovering the opposite sex. The boys didn't just hang out with the boys anymore. Spin the bottle was becoming more popular than kick the can.

But romance wasn't restricted to the young folks. Martha Dick and William Bones were together again, and this time, it would be for good. They began to see each other often, and were ready to start over as one united family. In 1966, they were married.

Martha Dick might have been ready to start over, but were her children?

For them, the marriage of their mom to her old high school flame would force another big shake-up in the family, and they still weren't completely over the last one. They would be told to share their mom with a new man and to open up their home to three new siblings.

Besides, if those weren't enough traumatic changes for the youngsters, they would also have to depart their beloved Denver. William Bones made his living in Michigan, and that was where the family was headed.

"I don't think he wanted to leave at all," recalled Rollie Bradford. "He had all his friends there, and had grown up there."

It didn't make any difference. At thirteen, Tim left the Mile High City for the Motor City, exchanging the comfort of his childhood companions and familiar frontiers for the uncertainty of a new family, a new school, and a new city.

Tim Dick was going on the road, and it wouldn't be the last time.

4

It was 1967 when the Dicks arrived in Detroit, looking for peace and stability in a new environment. They couldn't have picked a worse time.

The Motor City was about to go in reverse. Like Watts and Newark, Detroit turned into one of the nation's urban battlegrounds for America's raging civil war between blacks and whites. The black underclass, disenchanted with its lowly economic, social, and political status in society, rose up to knock down the symbols of the dominant white power structure. The city burned for days that summer, causing property damage in the millions, and resulting in forty-three deaths. When the smoke had cleared, Detroit would never look the same again.

The new family was fortunate to settle down in the safe suburb of Birmingham, a whole world away from the carnage near downtown. With its picturesque, tree-lined streets and immaculate neighborhoods, Birmingham made it much easier for Tim and his siblings to forget about Denver and the old gang. This new life might not be so bad after all.

Furthermore, Detroit served as the headquarters of America's thriving automobile industry, which meant that Tim, as he grew up, would be going to the same parties and attending the same schools as the sons and daughters of the highest-ranking auto executives. He would be able to examine his passion up close, and share it with others who were just as committed. If he had to move anywhere, it might as well be Detroit.

He attended Seaholm High School, which, like the rest of Birmingham, was mostly white and well-to-do. Seaholm provided the budding comic with his first big audience—the class of 1971 entered in the fall of 1968 with 723 students.

It was a class that mirrored the rapid, progressive changes in society. Since this was high school, not college, students didn't march in to take over the principal's office or stage massive protests against the Vietnam War. But the class of '71 did help make sure the campus fit in with the times.

Girls, for the first time, were allowed to wear slacks to school, and seniors could be excused from first and sixth hour study hall and didn't have to take gym. The class also planned the first Seaholm teach-in on pollution, encouraging students to collect empty bottles for recycling.

Tim and a few of his closest friends, however, were more interested in bottles that were full. Of beer, naturally.

"We'd get beers and take them to this beach, which we nicknamed Barf Beach because a few people chucked on the beach," recalled Michael Souter, a high school friend. "We crowned, 'Miss Barf Beach,' and then we would take the boats back and try to camouflage our breath from our parents."

Meanwhile, in the classroom, Tim returned to his familiar role as the prankster, and he had no trouble finding others to play along.

Nobody was immune from his sharp wit, though once again, just as in Denver, not everyone in his circle always appreciated it. "Sometimes you wanted to hit him," one classmate recalled. "He spent a lot of time apologizing when he said something to someone that hurt their feelings."

For the most part, however, his humor was pretty harmless, and was designed to court attention and approval, which is exactly what he received. Most of his friends thought he was hysterical.

"He used to like to do a lot of skits," recalled Amy Hursley. Whenever Tim was able to attract a small audience, she added, "he'd start making tons and tons of jokes, and they would all kind of roll together. You were just completely outwitted all the way through. You'd have to walk away because there was nothing more that you could do."

He was equally skillful at mimicry. "He used to always imitate his mother, his sister, and other girls," Souter recalled. "He had one great one for my mother who screeches when she talks. He would exaggerate all the right notes." Even as a teenager, the relationship between the sexes comprised a key part of his act. "We used to make a lot of women lib jokes," Souter added. "He imitated other girls, making fun of their hair and how they whine."

Tim reveled in his role as the class cutup, and never wanted to relinquish it. "If there was no opportunity for me to be a smart-ass," he told *People* magazine in 1992, "then I wouldn't be happy."

It came as no surprise, then, when Tim was selected by his classmates as the master of ceremonies for Swingout, the school's annual variety show that took place during graduation week. He was probably the Seaholm student who could think quickest on his feet, and, besides, as one friend put it, "He was the only one with the guts to do it."

Despite his comedic talents, however, Tim Dick was not known for being overly ambitious in high school. He didn't go around unveiling his master plan for the future.

Like most teenagers, he didn't have a master plan. He was an average student, the type of teenager who, like so many anonymous others, drifts through high school and is never heard from again. "He was one of the guys," said John Leaver, Seaholm's former vice principal. "He never stood out."

For that matter, Tim didn't even stand out in his own home. "It wasn't like you had a

great piano player in the house," Bill Bones
said. "He didn't keep the house in stitches all
the time."

Friends don't recall Tim ever talking seriously about any aspirations for a career in entertainment. Making people laugh in high
school was one thing. Making a living out of
it in the real world would be quite another.

But the show business dream must have
been hiding out somewhere in the class cutup's mind. One day, out of nowhere, he made
a rather bold prediction to Pete Shelley, who
sat in front of him in homeroom. "He said,
'Someday I'm going to be on the Johnny Carson show,'" Shelley said. "We were seniors
in high school, and I can remember it so
clearly."

Carson, a hero to Tim in adolescence,
would become almost a mythical figure to
him in adulthood. He would stand for the
fantasy Tim was always chasing, the elusive
life he prayed was not beyond his grasp.

First things first. Long before Hollywood,
there was Woodward.

Woodward Avenue is the main north–south
corridor between the suburbs and downtown,
which, like Sunset Boulevard in Los Angeles,
stretches from one entire way of life to another, from the upscale, secure shops of Birmingham to the decaying, crime-plagued
streets of Detroit. Tim and his middle-class
buddies, as expected, stuck mostly to the safe
part of Woodward, the burbs, which, nonetheless, provided their own sense of adventure—drag racing.

"We went nuts," recalled Cordell "Trigger" Craig, the undisputed king of the motorheads. "That's what we lived for, racing up and down Woodward to see who had the fastest car."

It certainly wasn't Tim. "Tim never really had a race car," Craig added. "He always hung with all those guys that did."

His peers, in many cases, raced with a distinct advantage. Their fathers worked for the Big Three automakers, which meant they could burn the pavement with the hot, or muscle, cars of that era—the Corvette, the Chevelle, the Roadrunner. Tim drove a Corvair. "We had one guy we called 'The Genius,'" recalled Craig. "His father was the vice president of General Motors. He had all this experimental stuff that we had read about in the magazines."

The races, often lasting until the early hours of the morning, became a ritual on Friday and Saturday nights. The girls showed up to root for their favorites, and afterward the whole group got together at the local burger joint to brag about the evening's results and make predictions for the next time.

Not all of the races took place on Woodward. The more hotly contested duels were staged on M-59, a new, relatively uninhabited stretch of highway where the cars could race for longer distances and at faster speeds. The trick, at both sites, was to stop traffic to allow the two teenage competitors, reaching as much as 110 or 120 miles per hour, enough time to drag a few hundred yards to the finish line.

It would be over in seconds. It had to be over in seconds. You could never be sure when the cops might show up.

It didn't matter that Tim was no genius. He was a motorhead, and Gerald Dick would have been extremely proud of his boy. Tim spent many hours devoted to the passion that has remained the one unwavering connection between his boyhood and his adulthood, between the beloved father who died too early and the brokenhearted son who carried on the tradition.

His stepfather, however, wasn't too wild about Tim's weekend nights on Woodward. William Bones was no Gerald Dick and never would be. "A car to me," Bones said, "I get in and turn the key. And boy, if it works, that's great, and other than that, I don't really care."

Bones and his wife explained to Tim how strongly they disapproved of his drag racing, but, not surprisingly, it didn't make a difference. Tim was a teenager with limitless energy and Bones was a stepfather with limited authority. Advantage: Tim. "I was not about to become the Grand Dragon," Bones said. "You take it very slowly. You have to have them build up their confidence in you."

Over the years, that would prove to be no problem. Tim would grow quite fond of his new old man. Ultimately, in fact, during Tim's most desperate hour, it was Bill Bones who rushed to his rescue. It was Bill Bones who provided the kind of compassion and conviction that helped turn Tim's life around before it was too late, and Tim would never forget it.

But that would be another lifetime away. What about the old man in Tim's former life, the father who departed without saying good-bye? What role did the memory of Gerald Dick still play in the mind of the boy who was trying to become his own man?

Nobody knew for sure except Tim, and he wasn't about to tell. Friends recall that he rarely brought up his late father, and he certainly didn't mourn in public for him. "It didn't seem to have that much of an effect on him because he was a very normal teenager and well liked by everyone," Bones recalled.

Then again, Tim's apparent emotional stability may have concealed a deeper, more painful reality. "I always knew that it (Gerald Dick's death) upset him quite a bit, but you have to realize in that era, even though it was the seventies, you didn't express your emotions that much," Michael Souter said. "It wasn't manly. We were all pretty waspy people. We'd keep things inside."

Tim didn't get a chance to reveal too much to the opposite sex, either. He was charming and went on dates, but he was never mistaken for the Fonz. "He didn't have the steady girl-friend with her arm around him, walking up and down the halls," recalled Hursley. "I think he was a bit shy that way."

Shy or not, Tim made it to the senior prom. His date was sophomore Eileen Murphy, and it wasn't the first time he had fallen for a Murphy. Tim had briefly dated Eileen's twin, Colleen, until she went steady with another guy. That's high school, where homeroom often lasts longer than romance.

"I thought they were kind of the Odd Couple," Hursley said. "She was real pretty, and it seemed like she would be with somebody who was a little more preppy, the Beach Boy type. Tim was more into being funny and hanging out with the guys than trying to impress the girls."

Tim spent the majority of his social life in a larger clique which, split evenly between boys and girls, ranked high on Seaholm High's all-important popularity ladder. They weren't the jocks, and they weren't the achievers, but, as one student put it, "They were probably close to the group to be with."

The group did almost everything together, including skipping school. "You'd have one of the girls that were in the crew write phony notes from Mom," said Pete Shelley, "and you'd be gone for half a day."

Overall, though, the gang engaged in harmless mischief. "We never did anything that I would call bad," Souter said. "We kept the teachers going. I think they were sad when we left because we were always doing something."

Tim also relished his membership in another tight group—the Saturday Morning Club, which met each week at Trigger Craig's house. Craig's father worked on Saturday mornings. With the adult conveniently out of the way, the kids took over. They watched one monster movie after another, played intense games of Foosball, and occasionally got stoned.

But high school couldn't last forever. Like the unique times they lived in, Tim and his friends, too, would have to do some changing. They would have to split up and grow up. They would have to embrace new causes and encounter new challenges.

They would have to leave Woodward Avenue.

The fall of '71 was coming, and the rest of their lives wasn't far behind.

5

College would be the first new challenge, which for many of the best and brightest Seaholm High grads meant attending either the University of Michigan in Ann Arbor or its rival, Michigan State University in East Lansing, the state's premier public institutions.

Tim Dick was not one of the best and brightest. He enrolled, instead, at Central Michigan University, which, nestled in the boonies about 150 miles northwest of Detroit, didn't carry the same credentials for academic excellence.

At first, Tim didn't seem to mind. He was not one of those impatient college freshmen, eighteen and already going on thirty. The real world could wait for a few years.

While he took a few courses in television production and even displayed a genuine interest in pursuing it as a career someday, the classroom seemed almost secondary to the other benefits college life could offer. "It was just one big party," said Shelley, his high school friend, and freshman roommate. "We all shouldn't have even gone to college together that first year."

Michael Souter was on campus, too, yet, if the temptation to resurrect the glory days of Seaholm High couldn't be fully satisfied by his Central mates, Tim would spend weekends in Birmingham or East Lansing. "It seemed like we were always going someplace," recalled Mark Klepper, his roommate during their sophomore year. "There was nothing to do at Central. It was in the middle of nowhere."

Tim tinkered with his stereo with the same care he used to tinker with his cars. "You just didn't have to have bigger speakers," Klepper added. "You had to have more of them." The sound blasting from those speakers often belonged to the J. Geils Band—Tim and his friends were Geils groupies. "They listened to rock-'n'-roll all the time," Souter said.

Soon, however, Tim began to face another type of music: It was time to leave Central.

He needed a school that could offer him more hands-on experience in television production. Central was Podunk, and Podunk wasn't good enough for him anymore. He was beginning to think bigger, which would become a lifetime habit.

He was also thinking about Johnny Carson again. "We'd watch 'The Tonight Show,'" Klepper said, "and many times, he'd say, 'I could do that. I could do that as good as he's doing that.' He always kind of talked about being a Johnny Carson."

Maybe so. Maybe Tim Dick could be the next Johnny Carson. But, first, he'd have to earn a degree before he could land a talk show. After his sophomore year, he transfered from Central to Western Michigan University in Kalamazoo. Tim was on the road again.

Western would prove to be a good and bad choice.

It was a good choice in the sense that it offered a top-notch television production department that gave Tim his first significant glimpse of a medium that would eventually become his livelihood. He fell in love with the camera, and the camera fell in love with him. He began to imagine how the serious social issues that take up space in his fertile mind could be explored in a much more dramatic fashion. He had found his calling, even if he wasn't aware of it yet.

Western was a bad choice, however, because it gave Tim his first significant glimpse of another side of life. It was in Kalamazoo where he became deeply involved in the dangerous world of drugs. He was not a complete stranger to that world—the Saturday Morning Club at Trigger Craig's house in Birmingham had made sure of that—but at Western Tim officially became its prisoner, and it would not be easy to escape.

In the early 1970s, *Playboy* had called Western Michigan University America's number one party school, and the label seemed to fit. The city of Kalamazoo was another typically conservative Midwestern enclave, but the student neighborhoods in town were sprinkled with counterculture relics from the late sixties, desperately clinging to causes and customs that didn't make the front pages anymore. Drugs, as always, comprised one element of that subculture.

"There was a lot of anti-Establishment protesting," recalled Professor Thomas Pagel, who taught communications. "It was like everywhere else in those days. Students felt they had a right to question almost everything."

On balance, though, especially in the beginning, Tim seemed very happy in Kalamazoo. He renewed ties with old friends, and made plenty of new ones. Most important of all, Kalamazoo is where he met his future wife, Laura Deibel.

She was a lot like him, rooted in the good life—her father, Gilbert, was a well-established attorney in Saginaw—and she owned a sense of humor, offbeat and irreverent, that could compete with his. Tim needed that in a girlfriend. His wit rarely took any time off.

Laura Deibel also possessed something even more vital than her humor and pedigree. She was fiercely loyal, especially to the man she loved, which Tim would never forget.

It quickly became clear to Tim's friends and family that Laura might be the one for him. "They were very comfortable with each other," Bill Bones recalled, "and they confided in each other. They discussed things you wouldn't normally do if it were just on a date."

Klepper also noticed a dramatic contrast between Laura and Tim's previous girlfriends, who, for one reason or another, didn't seem to stick around that long. "He seemed a little more serious than he had in other relationships," Klepper recalled. "He was one that girls wanted to be around, but not necessarily the one somebody would settle down with because, at that point, they'd be thinking, 'What's this guy going to do? He's just a joker.'"

That was certainly the case in Thomas Pagel's communications courses, in which Tim reprised his old role as the class cutup. Why not? He had the part practically memorized.

Yet for all their creativity, his jokes rarely disrupted the rhythm of the class. "In other words, he was not out to get you," Pagel said. "It was an exercise in his wit, in his fast response. If he thinks things are getting too heavy, he'll do it."

The class cutup, at times, however, could get pretty heavy himself. "He played down his intellectual capacity," Pagel said. "He tried to slough it off that he really didn't care all that much, and yet, when the work would come in, it would be generally better than you would expect."

The work was so outstanding, in fact, that Tim received a rare "A" from Pagel, and, in one particular case, left such a lasting impression on the professor that even today, twenty years later, he can still remember almost every detail. It was the final class project, in which students were asked to perform in front of the camera. Pagel hoped to demonstrate how television could create its own, unique reality.

For his monologue, Tim chose to put a move on an unsuspecting girl in class, only to discover, much to his amazement, that she already had a boyfriend and wasn't interested in him. He had never bothered to check his facts out first before letting his imagination and emotions go out of control. "It was probably the most disclosing of anything anybody ever did in my class," Pagel said. "The camera was a medium through which he was willing to open up."

In addition, the project in Pagel's class hinted at a developing theme in Tim's life that would gain more relevance as the years wore on.

"He seemed to always be a bit intrigued and bemused about relationships between men and women," Pagel said. "He was interested in the failures of communication," Pagel added, "and he wanted to somehow dramatize it." ABC would eventually give him a chance to do just that.

In college, Tim revealed, perhaps for the first time, the engaging, everyman look that would someday make him a star. Off camera he might be incorrigible, but on camera he was irresistible.

"You saw much of what there is now, the kind of playfulness and sense of telling with his face what he's feeling inside," Pagel added. "Some people have it, and some people don't. He had it."

But he didn't need the camera to make an impression. Tim, while not an especially well trained actor, seemed to know instinctively how to perform in front of an audience. "When we were in Improv Theatre," recalled Bill Ludwig, his roommate at Western, "he did an Improv of Hamlet all by himself, playing all the parts. It was great."

He knew how to write as well. Jules Rossman, who taught a television scripting course, said his "commercials were always far superior to anybody else's as far as creativity, originality, and humor. He had that spark of difference about him. I thought he would make one hell of an advertising copywriter."

Tim didn't confine his creativity to the communications department. He was an artist always working on his next creation.

Even designing furniture fit into his ever-expanding repertoire. His object of pride in those days was a folding swingback chair. "He was hoping he could sell a couple of them," Souter recalled. "He was really into three-dimensional design."

But all these other endeavors, from television production to copywriting to furniture design, were mere sideshows to Tim's true destiny in life. He was born to make people laugh. In Kalamazoo, by engaging in other creative distractions, Tim was still, consciously or not, attempting to defy that destiny. He didn't stand a chance.

He hooked up with WIDR, the type of alternative, almost-underground, campus radio station that separates college from the real world. Each week, Tim and another half dozen guys put together a thirty-minute anti-authority comedy show called "Five Finger Salute."

It was irreverent. It was topical. It was everything you never heard on mainstream radio. It emerged from a collection of zany oddballs who, whether the subject was drug abuse or gun control, were always looking to stir things up. The Sunday night show combined elements of Monty Python, National Lampoon, and Firesign Theatre.

Tim fit in right away. He was comfortable playing the outsider. It's another role he's never wanted to relinquish.

"He had such a quick mind that he could grasp a character and automatically come up with a speech or a line the guy would say," recalled one of the show's creators, Russ McQuaid. "We were all pretty quick guys because all of us had either gone into media or advertising, but it seemed like Tim was always about half a beat faster than everybody else. His comedic view of life was skewed toward the absurd. He'd see the hypocrisy in things."

In one sketch, Tim played the mastermind behind the government program to put the first Irish cop on Mars.

In another, he played a farmer whose cow was riding on surfboards down the middle of a small Illinois town. "You could tell from being with him that hopefully, this (his talent) was not going to stop here," McQuaid added,

"and that he'd find some way to make big
money someday."

The future once again belonged to Tim
Dick. He had a woman who loved him,
friends who adored him, and a family who
supported him. He had personality and talent.
He could go anywhere he wanted.

6

He stayed in Kalamazoo.

After earning his bachelor's degree in television production from Western in 1976, Tim became another one of those college graduates who don't know when it's time to get out of town and get on with their lives. Kalamazoo represented his safety net, a world where he could still make his own rules and his own mistakes. He could play the eternal adolescent, the professional hanger-on, and nobody would give a damn.

He hung around Kalamazoo to make some money in graphic arts, another discipline he managed to excel in without too much difficulty. But he also hung around for another reason. He hung around to sell drugs.

None of his friends can pinpoint exactly when Tim turned into a drug dealer, or why. It remains a sore subject for them, even two full decades later, a distant past better left undisturbed, a minor blemish on a man's record that simply isn't relevant today, especially in light of all the wonderful things he has accomplished.

But it is very relevant. It directly addresses the emotional state of a seemingly well-loved, highly talented college graduate who had no reason to break the law. It made no sense, which is what makes it so relevant.

"I ended up in a continued fantasy—drugs," he later told the court after his arrest, according to the *Detroit Free Press*. "At the time, it was very 'chic' to have and use coke. Record shops had the neat supplies, new wave magazines extolled its virtues, and I became wrapped up in the cocaine cult."

The signs of his secret life must have been there. Either those who knew him best chose not to read them properly, or they didn't know what to do about them.

"You could tell there was a great strain on him," recalled Jini Dingman, a Seaholm friend who visited him occasionally in Kalamazoo. Even Tim's stepfather admits: "We should have known that something was up ... If we had looked harder, we could have seen it."

In numerous interviews, Tim has brushed off his life of crime as merely the act of an aimless youth out to make the big bucks.

"Forty grand a month. What wouldn't you do for that in college?" he told the *Washington Post*. "I knew I was wrong. Immediately, I wanted out of this so bad, but it's like the CIA in those old spy movies—it's real easy to get into and it's really hard to get out."

Actually, he was about to get out, according

to an old friend from Denver. "He told me he was done," the friend said. "It was over. One more deal, and that would be it." Maybe, maybe not. Another friend, who went to high school with him, insists that Tim planned to make many more drug deals in his future. "He was talking about making millions of dollars," the classmate said.

On October 2, 1978, Tim got into his Nova and drove to Kalamazoo Airport. It was there that he met a buyer named Mike, who, according to the *Detroit Free Press*, had $42,000 in cash to purchase a pound and a half of cocaine.

According to the *Free Press*, it was Tim's idea to conduct the transaction at the airport. He had stolen the idea from a television movie. Tim and his partner feared Mike might be a cop, so they hoped that by putting the cocaine in a locker, they could avoid any trouble if the police happened to find it.

But, as Tim quickly learned, real life wasn't the same as reel life. At the airport, he gave the locker key to his partner, who then handed it to Mike. It looked like a done deal.

The deal was done, all right, and so was Tim Dick. He and his partner had been right about their suspicions. Mike was a cop.

"The next thing I observed," Tim said later from the witness stand, according to the *Free Press*, "was a gun in my face."

The cop was Michael Pifer, an undercover state trooper assigned to the narcotics unit of the criminal investigative division in East Lansing. Tim was charged with one count of delivery of a controlled substance, and one count of conspiracy.

Pifer had been closely monitoring Tim's drug transactions for months. In August, he had purchased a few ounces of cocaine from Tim, but had decided not to arrest him immediately, hoping he would lead police to his source. Finally, two months later, there was no reason to wait any longer.

"We figured we had gone as far as we could at that time," Pifer said, "and we would gain nothing further as far as locating the source or buying from the source without getting some cooperation." Eventually, Tim would give them some.

First, though, the boy from the suburbs had to deal with another sobering reality—jail.

He was transported to a cell in the Kalamazoo County Jail, which he shared with a fragment of society that had very little in common with him. He came from money, they didn't. He was born with opportunities, they weren't. "After being in dope for so long," Pifer said, "you see real jerks, real lowlifes, and he appeared to be a middle-class American kid, a typical college kid."

But the world behind bars has a way of neutralizing the distinctions that exist in the free world.

Tim was now one of them.

Russ McQuaid, his irreverent colleague from the "Five Finger Salute" radio show, was one of the first to visit him in jail. McQuaid, as a reporter in Kalamazoo, knew his way around the legal system. He brought

Tim a copy of *Rolling Stone* and some moral support.

He encountered a much different Tim Dick from the one who used to portray imaginary characters over the airwaves.

"He was very tense and worried, and made it clear that he had screwed up big-time and really didn't know what was coming ahead of him," McQuaid remembered. "He said he was going to have to get an attorney, and figure some way to get out of the situation. Most of all, I remember just the look in his eyes of being scared and in deep over his head."

Bill Bones also visited him soon after the arrest, and came away with the same general impression.

"He was in a whole lot of trouble emotionally," Tim's stepfather recalled. "He was totally unnerved. He was goddamn scared. They're not real pleasant people in there. All of a sudden you lose everything. Everyone goes to the john in the center of the room. The only thing he could say, I don't know how many times he repeated to me, was 'just get me out of here. Get me out of here.' "

Bones got the message. In his position, though, he certainly had the right to ask all kinds of probing questions, to begin trying to sort out the mess that had become his stepson's life. How did it happen? Why did it happen? When did it first happen? But Bones was more concerned with doing just what Tim asked him to do—getting him out of there.

He quickly drove home to Birmingham to begin rounding up the bail money, which fortunately for Tim's sake wasn't too difficult.

Tim was a free man again, on his way back to suburban comfort, away from the terrifying world he had just visited. But bail only earned him a reprieve. Tim would be back, and the next time his family wouldn't be able to bail him out.

Bill Bones had another job to do, and this one would be a lot tougher. His wife, Marty, was down in Florida when he received word of her son's arrest. Bones decided right away that the news was far too painful to notify her by telephone. He needed to be at her side for emotional support when she learned that her son was an accused drug dealer. So he flew by himself to the Sunshine State. "That was a long trip, my friend," Bones recalled, "a long trip."

Once down there, he told her the whole story. In a matter of seconds, life, as the family had known it for the past decade, suddenly became transformed forever. One of its own was going to be put away, perhaps for good. "We didn't talk much for a couple of hours," Bill Bones recalled. "She was just numb." The couple returned almost immediately to Michigan to plot strategy.

The first few days might have been the roughest. "None of us knew what to say," he recalled. "The effect he had on his mother was devastating. It was a very bad time in her life."

It was also a very bad time for his friends, who were just as dumbfounded as his family.

Sure, Tim could get a little wild sometimes. Sure, Tim could make some bad decisions. But a drug dealer? Absolutely not. Someone must have made a mistake.

"No one ever explained it to me," said one of his closest high school friends. "I was mad, and I thought it was so disrespectful to his parents."

Someone had made a mistake, all right. It was Tim, and it was a mistake that threatened to sabotage his entire future. No one could be blamed for counting him out.

"I felt here's one of the most talented people I'd had and he probably would never be able to recover from it," said Thomas Pagel, his communications instructor from Western. "He thought he was pretty smart and could get away with things, and I don't think he had thought through what the consequences would be."

The consequences looked like they would be pretty severe. Tim had made the wrong move at the wrong time in the wrong state.

Just one month before his arrest, the state of Michigan had passed one of the toughest new antidrug laws in the country. It mandated a life sentence in prison without parole for any person convicted of delivering or conspiring to deliver 650 grams (1.4 pounds) or more of cocaine or heroin. Tim and his partner had exceeded that amount.

The seventies were coming to a close, and society was no longer willing to put up with the pushers and users who had turned America's cities into cesspools of drugs and violence.

It would be months, however, before Tim would be sentenced by the courts. Until then, he would have to deal with the judgment of an even more authoritarian presence. His parents.

It didn't take Bill and Marty Bones long to get over the shock of Tim's arrest. At first, they asked themselves all the questions loving parents ask when a son goes wrong, and they came up with few answers.

"Neither his mother nor I could put a finger on it," Bill Bones said. "It would be easy to say it was because his father was killed, but that happened a long time ago, and if you think about it, at eleven, how long have you known your father? I mean, really know him? Maybe six years. It has an effect, of course. Does it have a lifelong effect? I tend to doubt it."

But, instead of wasting time on events they couldn't change, Bill and Marty Bones focused their time and energy on the events they could change. That had always been their way. Tim's problems with the law represented "the biggest tragedy in our lives," as Bill Bones said, but he and Marty had plenty of experience with tragedy. They knew how to fight back.

The first thing the whole family did was pull together, or as Bones put it, "circle the wagons." Although Bill and Marty suspected that their other kids knew more about the seedy side of Tim's past than they did, they chose not to interrogate them about the matter. "It wouldn't do any good," Bones said. "We felt at the time that if they did know, they'd feel very guilty about not saying something about it. What purpose would it have served?"

The second thing they did was straighten out Tim's life. Tim moved in with them in Birmingham, and there was no question about who was in charge. Bill and Marty had made that decision right away.

"When he came back here, it was no fooling around. 'You're living here, and you do what we say. You come and go as we say.' Those were the rules, and there were no more tears shed at that point. There was never any argument about that, either. He was in no position to argue with anybody about anything," Bones said.

It's quite likely that Tim was relieved to let someone else, for a change, make the important decisions. He had made enough wrong ones to last a lifetime. Tim had certainly gotten along well enough with Bones, and had even come to admire him.

But, prior to his arrest in 1978, according to Mark Klepper, his Central roommate, Tim had maintained a safe distance from his stepfather. "He really appreciated what he was doing for his mom," recalled Klepper, "but it was more his mom's husband, as opposed to his dad." Not surprisingly, once Bones assumed a stronger role in Tim's life, it brought the two of them closer together. "Maybe if we had done it five years earlier, who knows?" Bones said.

His parents were not the only authority figures whose approval Tim needed to solicit after his arrest. He had to break the news to Gilbert Deibel and his wife, and he wasn't looking forward to it. Gilbert Deibel was his girlfriend's father, the well-connected Saginaw attorney who probably wouldn't be too happy to find out that his daughter's lover had been caught dealing drugs and was likely on his way to prison.

Rarely had Bill Bones found his stepson in such agony. "I can still remember him telling me, 'I'd rather take a beating than do this,'" Bones said. "But he did it." Apparently it went very well. "Her family was very, very understanding," Bones added. (Months later, before Tim's sentencing, in fact, when it came time for character witnesses to speak out in his behalf Gilbert Deibel wrote a highly complimentary letter to the court in Kalamazoo. "We have heard him in performance, and he has remarkable talent," he wrote, according to the *Detroit Free Press*.)

It was only fitting, of course, that Laura was at his side for that painful pilgrimage to see her parents. Laura Deibel has always been at his side.

When it became clear that Tim would probably have to do time, nobody would have blamed Laura for leaving him.

She had trusted him, and, if it were true—and only she and Tim can tell for sure—that Laura didn't know anything about his drug activities, then he had violated that trust. It would mean that he had lived a complete other life separate from hers, a life of drugs and money and deception. Perhaps, in some fundamental way, he was not the man she thought he was.

"Her sticking it out was pretty remarkable," Klepper said. "It would've been so easy not to be around when Tim got out. You didn't know if he was going to be gone for a year, two years, six years."

Or as another friend put it: "There weren't any kids at the time, and they didn't have to worry about splitting up property. Not too many people would have put up with that situation."

But, despite it all, she didn't take off. "I never even considered the other option," Laura told *USA Today* in 1991 when the story of Tim's drug-related past first became national news. "It was just the right thing to do." In a later interview with *People,* she said: "We loved each other. It was that simple."

Even Tim had trouble comprehending her sense of loyalty. "It's the most amazing thing, because she had no reason to," he told the magazine.

As the days and months wore on, Laura and the other key players in the Tim Dick drama started to implement the only possible strategy at their disposal: Damage control.

How that strategy played out before the court might well determine which prison Tim would be sent to, and for how long. Everything had to be carefully choreographed to make him look as pure as possible in the eyes of the court, to paint him as a good guy who simply made one bad turn, not an habitual drug dealer and user with no remorse for his actions.

He had to be perceived as the Tim Dick of affluent Birmingham, not the Tim Dick of the Kalamazoo drug culture.

One priority of damage control was finding Tim a job. As a responsible wage earner, he would automatically find himself one notch above many of the countless other drug offenders waiting passively for their day in court. It would demonstrate a genuine desire on his part to compensate for his past behavior, and it would keep him occupied enough so he wouldn't hang around the house all day to brood about his uncertain future. The more distractions he had, the better.

Through the help of some friends, Tim found work as a salesman for the Sportsman, an upscale sporting goods store in town. Opened in 1953, it sold mostly outdoor equipment such as backpacks, fishing rods, parkas, hiking boots, and cross-country skis. He didn't get paid that much, but then again, he didn't take the job for the money.

Tim proved to be very capable in his new occupation. He had "a good gift of gab," recalled Charles Wilson III, who ran the store, "an ability to keep customers occupied in terms of interest. He had a joke for everything." Rob Cowin, a friend from high school, said, perhaps only half-kiddingly, that if Tim "didn't know something about a reel and a rod, he'd make it up, and hey, I'd buy it."

His sense of humor also won over a stand-up comic named Eric Head. Head wandered into the Sportsman one day in search of a prop he needed for a Clint Eastwood impression. He picked up the prop, and a new friend. Eric Head would turn out to be one of the most important collaborators in Tim's comedic career.

"He was folding sweaters, straightening out sunglasses in the case, and vaccuming the carpeting," Head recalls. "I ended up talking to him for four hours. He was a smart-ass right off the bat, and I thought he was about the funniest guy I had ever met. I wasn't used to being waited on with such irreverence and sarcasm. It just killed me. I loved it."

Head was so taken by his new friend that he suggested an instant career move. "If I could do this, you could certainly do it," Head told Tim, referring to stand-up comedy. "You're a real funny guy. You better do it, because you're going to make a mistake if you don't." Tim didn't seem totally shocked by the idea. "He said, 'Well, I've always kind of thought about it,'" Head said.

Of course, Tim had a few other things to think about in those days. He tried as much as possible to cover up his emotions with humor—that was the Dick way, after all—but it didn't always work.

"He was obviously nervous about it, trying to keep as busy as possible," Wilson recalled. "He knew very well that he was going to

serve some time. It was just a question of
whether it was a short time with some proba-
tion or a longer period of time. He didn't
know whether he was going to be sent to
Jackson (the state prison) or an executive-
type facility."

The job at the Sportsman also solved another problem. Bill Bones wasn't too worried
about how to supervise Tim inside the house.
Outside the house was an entirely different
matter. At the store, somebody was always
around to keep close track of Tim to make
sure he stayed out of trouble.

Nonetheless, a few months as an upstand-
ing citizen would not make up for a few years
as a white-collar criminal. It was even a very
good possibility that Tim, because of Michigan's new strict antidrug legislation, would
be put away for life. The damage control team
needed to find another way to strengthen his
position before the sentencing, and they
didn't have much time.

The government came to the rescue. They
gave Tim a chance to turn state's evidence by
telling the police and prosecutors whatever he
knew about the drug business, which was
quite a bit. As a dealer, Tim came into contact
with people higher up in the whole network.
If he testified about their activities, there was
a good chance that the law might go much
easier on him.

Tim decided he would do it, but his cooperation posed some obvious dangers. "He was
very worried about what the higher-ups in
the organization might do to him," Bones re-

called. "We were all very concerned about his safety at that point. Those people played rough." The family, however, according to his stepfather, didn't try to talk Tim out of his decision.

In exchange for his testimony, which, according to the *Detroit Free Press*, helped to indict twenty other people on drug charges, and, a prosecutor said, had resulted in the conviction of four major dealers, the state agreed to drop the most serious charge against him. He would first be sentenced in federal court, which was likely to be more lenient than the state judicial system. Perhaps he would receive very little prison time, if any at all.

In the meantime, as he waited for his fate, Tim started to give more attention to the idea of trying stand-up comedy. He had made people laugh wherever he went—at Seaholm, at Western, and, now, at the Sportsman. Maybe he really could make a living as a professional comic. Maybe he could make conversation with Johnny Carson.

If he truly was serious about trying stand-up, his timing could not have been any better. Detroit, a comedy wasteland for years, was slowly starting to build a legitimate scene thanks to the relentless efforts of Mark Ridley, who turned rejection into the best thing that ever happened to him.

Ridley, after failing to get into film school at the University of Southern California, had returned to Detroit, and in January of 1979 he opened the city's first major comedy club,

Mark Ridley's Room of Comedy and Magic, in a restaurant basement.

He had been a frequent visitor to the new Comedy Store on Sunset Strip in Los Angeles, mesmerized by comedians such as Richard Pryor and Jimmy Walker, and figured that if it could work in L.A., it could work in Detroit. "I thought it was the greatest thing in the world," Ridley said. "I just thought it was a great idea to bring back to the Midwest."

Great idea or not, Ridley needed a steady supply of local talent to stand any kind of chance for success. Later, when the club would establish a reputation, he would be able to import the best acts from across the country, the Lenos and the Lettermans. But in the club's embryonic stage he had to settle for whomever he could land, and in those days, frankly, it wasn't much. "With some help from local disc jockeys and newspaper columnists," he said, "I was able to scrounge together about nine or ten aspiring comedians who were very raw and rough, and were the same acts I'd have every night at the club."

Still, it was a start, which was better than nothing. For years, Detroit comics had fled to New York or Los Angeles if they wanted to make it big. Now, at least, they would be offered a local stage to try out their best material, to find out if they possessed a gift for comedy or a gift for self-delusion or both. If they couldn't make audiences crack up in Detroit, it was unlikely they would be able to bring down the house anywhere else, either.

Gradually, word started to spread around

town that Ridley's club, which he soon re-named the Comedy Castle, was a lively new hangout, a refreshing alternative to the famil-iar assortment of blue-collar bars and trendy dance clubs that made up nightlife in the big city. It didn't cost too much, and it was a great place to bring a date. Just sit back and let the comics do all the work.

Tim heard about the Castle, too. One day, according to the *Free Press*, he even phoned Ridley to check out when he might be able to drop by and perform. Come in a few days for Open Mike night, Ridley suggested.

Out of the question. Tim got off the phone. He first needed to find his niche and his nerve.

Finally, equipped with both—he reportedly put together thirty minutes of jokes in his basement, even though he would need only five minutes' worth—Tim was ready to make his debut at the Castle. It certainly made more sense than anything else he had tried to do since college.

"I was always making wisecracks," he told *Ladies' Home Journal* in 1992. "The world seemed upside down and kind of crazy to me then, so I figured, why not put the two together?"

Furthermore, he couldn't have discovered a more appropriate distraction from his other anxieties. Being afraid of going to prison or afraid of being bumped off by resentful drug dealers made stage fright seem almost trivial. "I had a guillotine on my neck," he told the *Detroit Free Press*.

As he prepared to go on that first night, he paced and paced. And then he changed his life.

Bill Ludwig, his college friend who assumed the role of cheerleader and therapist that evening for the frightened comedian, will never forget Tim's opening performance: "He slayed them."

Perhaps he did slay them, even if his material on that opening night did not rank as the epitome of social or intellectual insight. He wasn't a Carlin spinning clever word phrases or a Pryor examining contemporary social conflicts. He was a twenty-five-year-old sporting goods salesman on borrowed time who talked about bee vomit, farting, and the Pillsbury doughboy.

"Hi, everybody. Wouldn't you just love to cook that little Pillsbury doughboy?" he asked the audience. "Set him on a cookie sheet, put him on time-bake at 375."

But his material that night is not important. The only thing that really mattered on that winter evening in early 1979 was that Tim Dick, after some prodding from friends and soul searching within himself, had finally embarked on the career path that would turn his whole life around. It was his calling, and he could avoid it no longer.

"Having no style, no nothing—it amazes me to think about it now," he told the *Free Press* six years later. "When you don't know what you're doing, you don't know what can't be done."

After his performance, Tim removed a

brown ceramic tile from the Comedy Castle floor as a souvenir—it now hangs on the wall of his office—from the night he would never forget.

It was the night he became Tim Allen.

7

He had to change his name. Tim Dick was, in a very real, metaphorical sense, a person already banished to the past, a wayward soul who never fulfilled his promise. Besides, he couldn't just go on stage and tell everyone his last name was Dick. It would doom his act before he could get to his first punch line.

Whatever he called himself, Tim was hooked. "At first, I was just trying to keep my own spirits up," he told *Ladies' Home Journal* in 1992, "but then I found out I could make people laugh.

"What made me decide to stick with it was when I went to see one of Richard Pryor's concert films. He made me laugh so hard that I felt ill. That's a wonderful thing to do to someone, make them laugh until everything bad is washed away and they feel refreshed. I wanted to do that to people."

Ridley was more than willing to give him

the chance. Tim was eager, energetic, and talented, and, in any case, the Castle couldn't afford to be choosy in those early days. "We didn't have that many comedians at that time," Ridley recalled. "So it was just whoever was available to work, I'd put them on stage."

Tim didn't take too long to stand out from the other Detroit comedians. The same natural charm and likability that had impressed Thomas Pagel, his college instructor, came across to club audiences, allowing Tim to get away with the most vile and vulgar material. It also made a huge difference that, while most of the others dressed casually—usually jeans and a sweater—Tim wore a suit, a clever touch which instantly adorned him with an image of professionalism and wholesomeness, even if his act was one of the dirtiest in town.

He was also starting to earn respect from his competitors, which was no small accomplishment. Comedy, after all, is a very small community inhabited by the most fragile and insecure of performing artists. The last thing any of their easily deflated egos can ever bear is someone else doing the job better than they do.

In Tim's case, however, the other Detroit comics couldn't get around the fact that, after just a few months, he already was establishing himself as one of the best. "Tim came right out of the box as one of the stronger acts in town," recalled comedian Tim Lilly.

Despite his growing popularity, Tim kept his day job at the Sportsman. Comics, except

for the headliners, weren't paid in the early
days, and besides, it still made good sense to
maintain the status quo until the sentencing.
He had to hold down a responsible job, and
a part-time gig as a stand-up comedian didn't
exactly fit that description.

Yet while he was selling fishing rods and
cross-country skis, he was also selling himself.
He would try out his new material on unsuspecting customers, and then stop by the club
at night, buoyed by his new circle of friends
and the destiny he had finally embraced. It
wasn't such a bad life.

His stock as a comic, in fact, became so
prominent that when some of his colleagues
organized a strike in 1979, Tim's support was
heavily solicited. The comics, tired of working
for nothing, took encouragement from their
counterparts in Los Angeles, who had
adopted the same stance at the Comedy Store.
If it was right in Los Angeles, it was right
in Detroit.

"With Detroit being a union town, we were
smart enough that we knew that if we put up
picket signs, people weren't going to go to
those clubs," recalled comedian Tony Hayes.
"It was the Detroit blue-collar mentality."

But Tim wouldn't go along with the program. He had his own program to follow.
"Tim was the first to cross the picket line,"
recalled comic Lowell Sanders. "One guy
wanted to fight him. He stood up in his face,
and everyone argued. Tim was scared as hell,
but he went in and did his show. And, after

Tim crossed, a couple of other people crossed, too."

At first, according to Hayes, some of the other comics considered Tim a traitor who had betrayed the group's cause, who appeared only concerned with protecting his own hide.

Hayes was just as offended, until he later found out why Tim had refused to go along with everyone else. Of course, Tim was concerned about protecting his own hide. He wanted desperately to keep his own hide out of any more trouble than it was already in. "He was getting ready to go to prison," Hayes said. "If I had been aware of his situation, I would have taken a different attitude because I really liked Tim."

Tony Hayes wasn't the only one who didn't know the whole truth about Tim Allen. Tim was eager to be recognized for his talents, not his tribulations.

When the story about his drug problems did come out, it was sobering news for a tight group of performers who, despite their natural, built-in competitiveness, had grown quite fond of him. "Because this was one of our brethren," Hayes said, "we just didn't want to believe that he'd be going to prison."

Their disappointment, however, according to one comic, also related to how Tim's troubles might set back their own careers. "We were smart enough to know that if Tim made it to the big time," the comic said, he "was going to reach back and help us."

Then, when they learned that Tim had

agreed to provide state's evidence to help prosecute other, more influential, drug dealers, "We were really freaked about that," Hayes added. "We were worried that they'd get out and do something to Tim."

They weren't the only ones worried about his safety. So was Tim. If the scene at the Kalamazoo County Jail had made such a frightening impression on him, how would he ever survive the same world on a much larger scale, and for a much longer period of time?

In all likelihood, he would be grouped together with criminals who had endured a much tougher upbringing, who would be stronger, both physically and mentally, than a pampered boy from suburban Birmingham. Within the hierarchy of prison society, Tim would surely be one of the inmates on the bottom, and in prison, of all places, that was not a good place to be.

"He was really scared," recalled comedian Leo Dufour, of Windsor, Canada, who said Tim even joked about the possibility of escaping across the border, "but he wouldn't do that because his parents put up the bond." (Tim may, in fact, have been considering the notion of fleeing the country quite seriously. As he told the *Detroit Free Press* earlier this year: "I would not have gone to jail for life over that.")

Bill and Marty Bones, meanwhile, were doing everything they could to keep Tim out of prison or at the very least make it a short stay.

They took several trips to Kalamazoo to

meet with their attorney, who, according to Bill Bones, wasn't doing enough for their son. Bones said he even wrote letters to friends who were members of the Michigan Bar Association, complaining about the lawyer's ineffectiveness. "But on the other hand," Bones concedes today, "I don't know what he could do because Tim was guilty, and that was that."

His friends also pitched in to help Tim's cause, even contributing some money for legal fees.

Trigger Craig, his old friend from Woodward drag-racing days, said he raised a few hundred dollars, though others believed that since Tim had been the one to profit from his drug dealing, he ought to be the one to pay for it. Or, as Rick Bach, another high school classmate, pointed out: "All of us were pretty young at the time. We had no money to give to Tim's defense fund."

Soon, it was October of 1979. It had been a year since Tim Dick and his partner had been arrested at the Kalamazoo Airport.

He had used that time very wisely. He had landed a new job and launched a new dream. He had drawn closer to his family, and, in many ways, closer to himself. He had finally become, at twenty-six, the kind of person he should be. The future looked bright.

But the future would have to be put on hold. Tim Dick still had to take responsibility for the past.

It was not easy for him to let go of his new life—it had been much better than the old one. He kept doing stand-up almost right up until his long-dreaded day in court.

In fact, according to an astonished Tony Hayes, Tim spent one of his last weekends of freedom at the Castle. "What are you doing?" Hayes asked him. "Tim, don't you want to be with your family? If I were in your position, I'm pretty sure I'd want to spend it with my family." Tim told Hayes he would see his family later, and, besides, he had to keep his routine sharp. Comedy, he hoped, was going to be his livelihood for a long time—once, that is, he became a free man again.

Yet, even as he mentally prepared for his time behind bars, Tim was able to find humor in the situation and shared it with his closest friends. "They were the kinds of jokes that would make you cringe," recalled comedian Mark Kornhauser, "jokes about getting raped in jail, about Bubba, Bubba being some non-descript big guy who's going to make you his Mistress."

Soon there was no more time to make jokes. Tim had to leave the Castle and his calling. He didn't want a big emotional scene at the end, and neither did the comics, each preferring to view the departure as temporary. "He said, 'Listen, I'll see you guys sometime soon,' " Ridley recalled. "He sort of took it in good spirits. There wasn't crying and hugging. He wanted to keep it kind of low-key."

A few comics, however, expressed some doubts that Tim would ever return to the stage. They had heard the familiar horror stories about the real Bubbas in prison life, and they knew that Tim wouldn't be any match for them.

But Ridley was always optimistic. From the beginning, he had believed in Tim, perhaps more than anyone ever had, and he wasn't going to lose faith now. "It was just sort of an extended vacation," he said. "It wasn't like he was going to Death Row."

Finally, in the fall of 1979, Tim received his punishment. First, he was given a five-year term by a federal judge. Then, a month later, he appeared before state Circuit Court Judge Patrick McCauley in Kalamazoo. In his statement to the court, Tim made one last appeal for a light sentence:

"I became involved in this as a pretty arrogant college kid and didn't have any idea of what I was getting into. I became an excessive user which led to the arrest which in a way was the slap I kind of needed to straighten things out in my head ... and without sounding cheap, I am really sorry for the trouble I have caused everyone, especially the mud I have pulled my parents through and stuff, but I think I can make a positive contribution to society, and I am just hoping that you look that I have no past record."

It was a good speech, and he probably meant every word of it. But Tim Dick would still have to pay for his crime. Judge McCauley sentenced him to three to seven years, to be served concurrently with the five-year term that had been imposed a month earlier.

The good news, however, was that Tim

would be allowed to serve his time in a federal prison instead of a state facility. "You might have some enemies there," Judge McCauley told Tim.

The judge also proved to be quite a prophet. He acknowledged Tim's considerable gifts as a comedian, and gave him a few words of advice:

"Don't waste it. It shouldn't be wasted . . . You can perfect your talents while you are in prison. When you come out, I expect to see you very, very successful as a comedian. I expect to see your name in publicity magazines . . . The last year you have been out, you have been training. You have been perfecting your abilities. Continue that, then, this hasn't been such a tragedy. If you don't continue, if you get in with the wrong crowd . . . then you will have wasted all of this."

Tim was taken away. Just like that, it was all over. "The marshals grabbed him, and got him out of there, one on each side of him," Bill Bones recalled. "He was pretty numb at that point."

His family wasn't feeling any better. The damage control strategy had worked up to a certain point, saving him from a life sentence. He would have a future someday on the outside.

But it could not spare him completely from the humiliating ordeal of incarceration. Good job or not, new outlook or not, state witness or not, the whole combination wasn't quite enough to make up for the past. Tim Dick was going to do some time, and his family could do nothing about it.

"She took it very hard," Bones said, referring to how Tim's mother reacted to the sentence. "She was very, very upset."

Needless to say, so was Tim. He came from a good family and had mastered the role of model citizen since his arrest. "I really didn't expect that they would give me as much prison time as they did," he told *People* magazine. "I was a college grad, and I'd made only one mistake. But [the court] didn't quite look at it that way."

Years later, in an interview with Barbara Walters, Tim went even further: "I never thought that I would get any time. I thought, a well-educated kid, I made a mistake, I admitted my error, I pleaded guilty, didn't want to take it to a trial."

Nonetheless, being in prison was a lot better than being dead, which is another way the Tim Dick story could easily have played out. "He once told me he was actually thankful that he got caught," Trigger Craig said, "because he figured that he'd either end up becoming so big that he'd do so many drugs and kill himself, or somebody would kill him."

Tim acknowledged the same point himself in a 1991 interview with *USA Today:* "In a hideous way, aside from the pain it put my family and friends through, getting caught probably saved my life. I used the facilities of prison to figure out what was important and moved on from there." Perhaps, on some subconscious level, Tim sensed it was the only way he could break completely free from both his risky lifestyle and his repressed anger. "Doing it was dumb," he told *TV Guide*. "I was asking to get caught, I think."

In any case, Tim was soon on his way to the Sandstone Federal Correctional Institution in Sandstone, Minnesota, a low-security facility that housed a few hundred inmates. It could have been a lot worse. "He was relieved when he found out it was a federal penitentary, where everyone else in there wasn't a murderer or rapist," said comic Mark Kornhauser. "They were a little bit more white collar."

If Sandstone was no Sing Sing, it was no country club, either. He would still have to face the society he had dreaded ever since his arrest a year earlier. He would run into roughly the same caliber of characters he had encountered at the county jail, and it was a pretty good possibility that they would make trouble for a spoiled kid from the other side of the tracks. He wasn't one of them, and they would know it soon enough.

This time, Tim wouldn't be able to get bailed out by a loving family and a loyal girlfriend. He had created his own nightmare, and he was the only one who could save him.

8

Judge McCauley was exactly right about Tim Dick. He did have two choices.

Either he could use his time behind bars to chart a whole new course, or he could repeat the mistakes of the old one. It was up to Tim.

He would have plenty of time to decide. Prison, for all its degradations, does offer the incarcerated an opportunity to reflect, to pause from the relentless rhythm of the outside world and recognize with sometimes painful clarity the rocky path that he or she has just traveled. It can be, ironically enough, the most liberating experience of all.

Tim, to his credit, had already exorcised some of his demons before he put on his prison uniform. He had admitted to himself—and the court—one of the reasons why he had turned to drugs, and it wasn't just for the money, as he would contend in later years. It was far more complicated than that.

The Tim Dick at twenty-five still seemed to

be mourning the life which had been abruptly taken away from him fourteen years earlier by a drunk driver on a Colorado highway. "Since my father was killed, I have not been directed," Tim said in a statement to the court after his arrest, according to the *Detroit Free Press.* "I had trouble taking things seriously. I was afraid of working and failing in the real world."

For a year after his arrest, however, Tim had worked in the real world, and this time, he had not failed. He had started to straighten out his life, and he was taking things extremely seriously.

Even so, the new Tim Dick was not that far removed from the old one. A year was not enough time to officially qualify him as a new man. He first had to pass a number of tests, and prison was at the top of the list.

From the first day of his incarceration, Tim recognized that he wasn't going to get by in this scary subculture without a game plan, and brute strength wasn't going to be it. He needed another weapon, one that he would be able to rely on at the most pivotal moment, such as when a fellow inmate might threaten to pound him all the way to Minneapolis.

So he wisely turned to the most dependable part of his limited arsenal—his humor.

Just as he had employed it to disarm and manipulate the most insensitive kids in elementary and high school, who poked fun at his last name, Tim used it to disarm and manipulate his fellow inmates at Sandstone. "Humor was the only defense I had," he told

People magazine in 1992. "Two minutes after I was there, I started babbling. So everyone knew I was a geek right away."

In his book, he relayed the story of how he would quickly babble like the cartoon character Elmer Fudd to keep one overmuscled inmate from pummeling him. "You could kick butt anytime," he wrote, "but you don't get to laugh that much in prison. It proved very valuable to me." To get the guards on his side, Tim, according to *Time* magazine, put pictures of Richard Nixon in the peephole of his cell.

Tim also found it valuable to use some acting skills. "He said that one of the first days you're in there, you have to act like you're crazy," said high school friend Rick Bach. "Otherwise, he said, they'll take advantage of you. He would say, 'If you touch me, I'm going to have to kill you, or at least die trying.'"

As time went on, Tim realized his humor could serve another purpose in prison. He was determined to get his act together—literally.

Judge McCauley had told him he could "perfect his talents" in prison, and the judge had a good point.

After all, why should Tim allow something like a federal penitentiary to get in the way of his rising comedic career? Besides, in prison he wouldn't have to worry about drawing a large enough crowd. This was one crowd which he knew wasn't going to have other plans. All Tim needed, then, was a stage, some fresh material, and he'd be ready to go.

Well, not exactly. He still had to convince prison authorities to go for the idea. "I remember it took quite a lot to set it up, and he didn't get a lot of support for it," recalled comic Mark Kornhauser, who helped Tim with the special gig.

Kornhauser, who performed a comedy/magic act, made frequent stops at college campuses in Minnesota, so it wasn't too difficult for him to fit in a trip to Sandstone. "The prison staff was concerned," he said. "They had to have security. Anything that was a break in the routine for the guards was a potential threat."

Finally, Tim got through the red tape. Now he would just have to get through the performance.

It turned out to be more difficult than he ever imagined, and it wasn't because he was rusty in front of an audience, which he undoubtedly was, or because he hadn't spent enough time fine-tuning his material.

As Kornhauser remembers it, Tim had a tough time because he had misjudged his audience. He had failed to keep in mind that he wasn't performing anymore in front of satisfied suburbanites who could appreciate it when a comedian poked fun at their vulnerabilities. He was performing in front of patrons far from satisfied with their fate.

"Tim had written a lot of stuff about being in prison," Kornhauser recalled, "but the prisoners didn't really like it at all. It was a little too close to home for them to laugh at it. It's possible you can laugh at something like that if you know you're getting out in a while, but some of those guys were in for life. They were pretty hard-core. I think had he done a normal stand-up routine, Tim would have done much better."

For his punishment, Tim was handed a comic's worst sentence—silence—and there wasn't a thing he could do about it. "He was squirming," Kornhauser said. "He very early recognized that they weren't buying this, yet he was committed to do what he had written, and had to go ahead with it."

The crowd warmed up a little bit for Tim when he told some nonprison jokes, Kornhauser said, and, overall, he was grateful to get the opportunity to perform again, whatever the venue. Being away from his new love—the stage—was one of the worst parts of being locked up. "It gave him a taste of what he really wanted," Kornhauser said, "regardless of how he evaluated it. I just think it meant a lot to him."

After the show, Tim escorted his friend to the prison exit. Throughout the day, Kornhauser had received the impression from Tim that he was coping as well as could be expected in such a hostile environment. He had made friends and had stayed away from enemies. He was pumping up his muscles and his spirits.

But, on his way out of Sandstone, Kornhauser stared back at Tim for the last time, and his expression revealed something else entirely. Even today, about fifteen years later, it's a look Kornhauser can still recall vividly. "This big iron door slid between us," he said. "He was on one side and I was on the other, and he looked so forlorn. It was very sad."

No wonder Tim looked so forlorn. Just moments earlier he and Kornhauser had both performed on the same stage, equals as artists and as human beings.

But they weren't equals. Kornhauser was headed back to civilization. Tim was headed back to his cell. "He loved performing, and he knew right on the other side of that steel door was his life," Kornhauser said.

Still, as painful as it was to be separated from the destiny he had finally claimed, Tim chose not to live in denial.

He called the Castle's Mark Ridley at home once a month for an update on the Detroit comedy scene. "I kept him appraised of who was doing what," Ridley said. " '[Dave] Coulier's in L.A. and things are going well for him.' He was chomping at the bit. He couldn't wait to get back."

Even behind bars, hundreds of miles away, it was important to keep track of his competition, and, in a way, perhaps, to remind them—and himself—that, someday, he would be back. "He was really worried that people would have forgotten about him," said comedian Leo Dufour.

Tim's loyal girlfriend, Laura Deibel, did whatever she could to make sure that didn't happen. She dropped by the Castle on occasion to catch a few acts and report back to

Tim, though it must have been painful for her to be at a place with so many memories of her imprisoned boyfriend. "She looked really depressed," Tony Hayes recalled. "She would just sit there some nights. It was sad."

Her devotion made quite an impresson on the comics. "You're looking at a woman who came from money," Hayes added. "Laura's people are very well off, so it wasn't like she was with Tim for the dough." As another comedian, however, pointed out: "She obviously believed in him that someday it would pay off."

Depressed or not, Laura summoned the courage to deal with Tim's confinement. The same can't be said for all of the Detroit comics. Just as he had feared, many of them had forgotten about him.

"With the exception of Sheila Kay, basically everyone kind of let Tim rot in prison," said comedian Tim Lilly. "No one really kept any kind of contact with him, none of the comics, anyway. The comics basically went, 'Well, that's one less guy we have to worry about as far as competition.' "

Tony Hayes said it had nothing to do with competition and everything to do with compassion. The comics shied away from Tim, he claims, precisely because they *did* care for him. "We just blocked it out," he said. "A lot of guys were afraid they'd never see him again." Some, he added, were even upset when they didn't get a chance to participate in the special show at Sandstone. "I think it was because we never got the correct information about it," Hayes said.

Not everyone forget about him. Other friends corresponded regularly with Tim, both by letter and phone.

"The main thing he talked about were women and how 'it really sucks in here,'" recalled Trigger Craig, "but the one thing that rings out in my mind is him talking about this one Colombian who didn't speak English, and how they put him in with a bank robber from America, and the first thing he taught him was, 'Put the money in the bag, and don't touch the alarm,' and that's all the guy said around prison."

The majority of Tim's friends, however, found him in an optimistic mood. "We would constantly write each other letters," said Eric Head, "about how one day, when we had our own production companies and were producing feature films and television shows, we would each have our own secretaries.

"He would write me and tell me what his office would look like, and I would tell him what my office would look like. We said we wanted the hippest lobby in the world. It would not have any chairs to sit in, a male secretary at a podium, and we thought that would be the ultimate, that you'd have no place to sit when you came in."

Tim refused to feel sorry for himself. Judge McCauley had told Tim to take his punishment like a man, and, once again, he was going to do what His Honor said.

"He never wrote a bluesy-type letter," re-

called Bill Bones. "As a matter of fact, he just
took it all in stride."

So, after a while, did his family. Marty
Bones was never one to stay too down for too
long, or, if she did, she certainly wouldn't
show it in public. When Gerald Dick died,
"She might have mourned him for twenty-
four hours," Bill Bones said, but "beyond
that, nobody knew."

At large family gatherings the conversation
didn't automatically switch over to Tim and
his troubles. There were eight other brothers
and sisters with lives to share.

"Frankly we didn't discuss it a whole lot,"
Bill Bones said. "We didn't sit around and
wring our hands. It was so painful there was
no sense stirring the whole thing up. It was
just a done deal by then. He would serve his
term, make the best of it, get out of there, and
get on with life."

But their strength couldn't cover up their
sadness. Underneath the surface the thought
of Tim "was always there," Bill Bones said.

Mercifully, time passed. The days turned
into weeks, the weeks turned into months.
Tim, as far as the family could surmise from
their conversations on the phone with him,
appeared to be coping well with his new sur-
roundings. "We always had the obvious dis-
cussions about how he was getting along,"
Bones recalled, "about the food, and whether
he got enough exercise." But Bones didn't pry
into anything deeper than the basics, "and he
didn't offer."

Finally, in February of 1981, Tim was moved from Sandstone.

He wasn't a free man just yet—his next stop was a halfway house in downtown Detroit. He would be placed on parole for five years, and the stigma of being an ex-con would never totally go away.

But Tim had done what many, including himself, wondered if he could do. He had survived eighteen months in a federal penitentiary.

"There are obvious dangers in prison," he told *TV Guide* in 1991, "but I wasn't as weak as I thought I was. I got through it. And when I got out, I was still a young man. I had plans and I was ready."

Judge McCauley had told him he had two choices. By the time Tim had served his sentence, it was clear which choice he had made. Like Malcolm X, Tim Dick used prison to start over.

"Prison was the worst and the best thing that ever happened to me," he wrote in his book. "It taught me in no uncertain terms to be responsible for your actions."

9

His new home was no prison, but it was no paradise, either. Located in the living quarters of the former St. Peter's Lutheran Church across the street from Tiger Stadium in downtown Detroit, the halfway house served to facilitate Tim's re-entry into the outside world.

He was free to leave each day but had to return by a certain hour in the evening. "It was a very grim place," Bill Bones recalled. "It was kind of dark and dingy, in an old building, in not the best part of Detroit."

It was in the part of Detroit that Tim and his high school crowd had mostly avoided during their cruising days down Woodward. But Tim was no longer the sheltered son of privilege. He was a man who had seen the worst and lived through it. Nothing fazed him anymore.

Once again, his first job was to put his life back together. This time, though, he would start out from a much better position than he had immediately after his arrest in the fall of 1978.

Since then, he had picked up valuable experience in the working world, as a salesman and a stand-up comic, and he was no longer operating on borrowed time. He was, exactly as he envisioned himself, a young man who had plans.

Plan A, no doubt, was to resume his career as a comedian. While his involuntary sabbatical had forced him to sacrifice important ground to some of his less talented contemporaries, who were playing the hottest rooms in the country, the time away from the stage, ironically enough, probably did more to nourish his dream than to starve it.

In captivity, he began to truly grasp, for the first time, the total commitment it would take to make it as a stand-up comic. Putting together a good act wouldn't be nearly enough. He would also have to work harder than he had in his entire life. "Prison gave him the big kick," said Seaholm classmate Michael Souter. "Tim always did a lot of stuff in college, but he never had the big kick. We were all taken care of by our parents. We did things to a certain extent, but we never had to fight real hard for them. We just took a lot for granted."

At the same time, Tim realized that it would be premature to invest all his time and energy in such a precarious profession as comedy. He needed to make a living, too, just in case he didn't turn out to be the next Lenny Bruce.

He went back to the Sportsman. The pay

wasn't too good, about $110 a week, but it provided him with a supportive working environment, and, another opportunity to experiment with his freshest material. If he bombed with this audience, it wouldn't matter anyway. He could just try again the next day in front of other customers.

He also knew he was not going to be a salesman for the rest of his life. Reformed or not, Tim Allen or Tim Dick, he required an outlet for his creativity and unique slant on the world. Selling backpacks and cross-country skies to outdoor-minded suburbanites wasn't exactly what he had in mind.

Tim chose advertising, a field always looking for fresh talent with a different point of view.

Shortly after he got out of Sandstone, he got a job at a small advertising agency in downtown Detroit run by two Seaholm classmates, Rick Bach and Donald O'Connor. The firm did work for Uniroyal Tires.

"He came down to the office, and kicked around for a couple of hours," Bach said, "If we paid him, it was very little." If Tim held any title, Bach added, it would have been as an assistant copywriter. "All we were doing, basically, was writing scripts for slide presentations about tires, boring stuff."

In any case, Tim seemed happy to hang around with old friends and talk about new dreams. He might make the occasional joke or two about his experiences at Sandstone, yet for the most part he was extremely anxious to leave his past behind, and nobody could blame him. He had a future that had been delayed too long.

Sometimes, though, the past wouldn't cooperate with his agenda, and there was little he could do about it.

One day, Bach recalled, a frantic Tim arrived in the office with a letter that he insisted had to be notarized immediately. "It was about his past activities," Bach said, "about the people who were going to be mad at him. Tim had written down all this stuff, that, if he were harmed in any way, this is what was going on." Tim brought the letter to a woman who worked as a notary in the same building, Bach added, but once she had read it over, "She wanted nothing to do with it."

Over time, Tim learned how to deal with fears about his personal safety. The drug dealers he had turned in were not coming to get him.

He also learned how to deal with his anger. In prison he had wisely directed it toward himself, accepting full blame for his actions and for the pain he had put his girlfriend and family through. He was going to do his time and get the hell out of there.

But once he was out he said he became angry when he discovered the same situation he had left behind eighteen months earlier.

"Nothing had changed," he told the *Los Angeles Times* years later. "I thought if I was to be made a lesson, if I had come out and somehow magically, the (nation's) cocaine problem would have disappeared . . . but the problem was getting nothing but worse, and I felt guilty about being part of that problem."

The new Tim, however, bolstered by the support of his family, the loyalty of his girlfriend, and perhaps, above all else, by the love of his profession, wasn't going to be defeated by any emotions. "I was glad I had comedy to turn to," he told *Ladies' Home Journal*, "because I didn't want to become bitter or angry. That's an important part of making it once you've done your time."

Tim had done his time, all right, and now he was ready to do more time—on stage. His good friend Mark Ridley had assured Tim in those monthly phone calls that he would keep a spot open for him whenever he got out of Sandstone, and Ridley kept his promise.

The other comics couldn't wait to see if it was the same old Tim. "We were all glad to see him back," said Tony Hayes. "Here was a guy that had started with us and had gone away, and he had worked all of that out, and he was back."

It wasn't the same old Tim. It was a better Tim. "He got on stage, and seemed a little nervous, but he did a great job. It was basically the same stuff he had done before," Hayes added, "except that he seemed more lively. There's no doubt he had worked on his act."

He certainly didn't have time to waste. When Tim first performed on stage in early 1979, the comedy scene in Detroit, as well as throughout much of the nation, was only beginning to emerge as a significant entertainment force. Until the strike, comics didn't even get paid. The Comedy Castle was the only game in town.

By late 1981, it was an entirely different game, both in Detroit and across the country. Many clubs and bars had undergone major overhauls to become comedy venues. "He had been out for two years," recalled comedian Jerry Elliott, "and the two years that he was gone, you saw probably three or four more clubs open locally, and, more importantly, clubs opening nationally. There were enough clubs open for people to quit their day jobs and go full-time stand-up."

In the beginning, Ridley didn't rush Tim to become a headliner. Instead, he made him the opening act for some of the more well known comics from out of town. The Castle was beginning to acquire a reputation from coast to coast, drawing such major talents as Jay Leno, Jerry Seinfeld, and Paul Reiser. "Tim was trying to get reestablished," Ridley explained. "He was experimenting with his act. It was a chance for him to work out."

Even a rusty Tim Allen was better than many of his well-oiled competitors. He was so good right away, Ridley said, that other comics begged him, " 'Don't put him out in front of me. He'll blow me off the stage.' " Comics have always been afraid of being blown off the stage by the act in front of them. It is challenging enough to come with original material, an innovative delivery, and an appealing character, without having to worry about somebody else.

"He'd do a little guest spot of ten minutes," Elliott said, "and then he'd go for fifteen, twenty minutes, blow the room out, and then the headliner is going, 'What just happened?' Tim liked to do that because it really put the spotlight on him. The good headliners never had a problem. The guys that bitched the loudest were the guys who he buried."

No wonder some of the national comics were jealous. Here was a relative newcomer to their sacred profession who was already doing much better than guys who had been toiling in the clubs for years. Everyone knew only a handful would ever make it big. The rest would play every Holiday Inn from Albany to Anchorage.

But most of the Detroit comedians didn't care about the extra competition. They were just thankful to see Tim back on the stage. Their buddy had survived Bubba.

Some, however, were a little ashamed because they hadn't corresponded more regularly with him when he was behind bars. "He was hurt," Hayes said. "He said, 'You guys didn't even write me.' We all felt bad."

Tim's act offstage was also better after prison. "Even though we were all around the same age," Hayes added, "Tim became more mature, more fatherly. He would tell guys not to go on the road and pick up women, and not to hang out with the wrong element."

Tim definitely had to keep a safe distance from the wrong element. He was still an ex-convict on parole, and another mistake could land him back in the slammer, and, this time, he couldn't be sure he'd get out so quickly. He had already invested too much into his rehabilitation to squander it in a moment of temptation or weakness.

His family, too, was concerned about any potential relapse, so that when he was let out of the halfway house after a few months, Tim moved right back in with his parents in Birmingham.

Once again, Bill Bones was the man in charge, and the household rules remained just as rigid as they had been the last time. Tim still had a lot to prove to his parents, and to himself. "There would be no nonsense, no riding up and down Woodward Avenue at seventy miles an hour," Bones said. "He accepted all that. He didn't step out of line an inch."

Tim, according to Bones, wasn't quite as understanding about the rules that related to his parole. He could accept his family playing the enforcer, but not his government.

"He was troubled that he couldn't do this or he couldn't do that," Bones said. "It was more of a nuisance than anything else, little things, like he couldn't go to Canada." (That restriction, incidentally, prevented him from doing his stand-up routine at the Komedy Korner, a comedy club across the river in Windsor owned by his friend Leo Dufour. "He really wanted to play that room," recalled comedian Al Aprill. "It was a neat room at the time.")

Tim was tested constantly and passed each time. He was a new man all right. "After the shows, guys would get together out in the parking lot and smoke joints," Aprill said. "Tim would be part of that, but because of just being out of prison, he couldn't really partake. I'm sure he wanted to be one of the boys, but he had to back off. He was always backing off."

Not always. He still had a weakness for fast automobiles. "We had just done this gig in Holly," Hayes recalled, and "I noticed that Tim was really going fast, maybe eighty, ninety miles per hour. We drove about ten minutes like that. He likes to live on the edge."

But, for the most part, Tim had too many plans and too little time to live on the edge. The edge had robbed him once already. "He was in it (comedy) for the art," recalled comedian Bruce Baum. "He wasn't into it for the party."

Tim had survived prison and the grim halfway house. He had begun to regain the trust of his family and friends.

He had rejoined society and the working world, and he had reclaimed his rightful role in the comedy community.

He had redeemed the reputation of Tim Dick, and now he was ready to make a new one for Tim Allen.

10

Tim Allen did not have a confidence problem. Prison may have taught him many lessons, but humility was not one of them.

"If he was cocky going in," Jerry Elliott said, "he was really cocky coming out."

Perhaps, by emerging relatively unscathed from his daily encounters with the worst society has to offer, Allen had come to believe that he was capable of surviving any challenge, and that somehow it was his superior spirit and will that pulled him through.

If that were true, he would need to call on every ounce of his strength for the equally daunting task of surviving in show business. It was one thing to triumph over a crew of journeymen comics in a provincial entertainment town like Detroit. It would be quite another to become a star.

What did Tim Dick want anyway? He wanted it all, according to Mark Ridley. "Like everyone else, Tim had a plan," Ridley re-

called, "and part of it was to be on 'The Tonight Show,' and then to get on his own
sitcom and do movies." One night, at a local
restaurant, "I remember one of the comedians
going, 'Well, those are awfully big plans,' and
Tim was adamant, 'Well, I'm going to do it.' "

He was perhaps most adamant about getting on Carson. Ever since high school, he
had talked about it, and now that he had
actually become a professional comedian,
the idea wasn't as farfetched as it might
have first seemed. Carson, in the early eighties, still symbolized the epitome of success
for a stand-up comic. If you could do a
few good minutes in front of Johnny, Ed,
Doc, and the band, you had a chance to
become famous.

Those who knew him the best didn't
doubt that he was headed for the big time.
"Everyone knew he was going to make it,"
said George Kutlenios, who runs a comedy
room at the quaint Holly Hotel, about
twenty-five miles from Detroit. In the early
eighties, Kutlenios figured, of the sixty or so
comics working regularly across the state,
Tim was the one most likely to make it to
Hollywood.

He was already too late to be the first. Detroit alumnus Dave Coulier, who was signifi-
cantly younger than Tim, was playing the top
clubs in Los Angeles, getting plenty of work
in voice-overs, and doing animation for Nick-
elodeon. Later, Coulier would acquire a long-
running starring role on the ABC-TV hit sit-

com "Full House." This time, it was Tim's turn to be jealous.

"That was the big thing, move to L.A.," comedian Leo Dufour recalled, "and when Coulier did it, it kind of bummed him out because he beat him to it. We used to call Dave 'Star baby.' We used to watch him on stage, and draw pictures with helicopters with Dave flying in them, waving good-bye. He made it big real quick, and we were all envious."

Coulier often returned to Detroit to rave about life in Los Angeles and the opportunities it presented him. "He'd tell us the great stories," recalled Ken Calvert, a Motown disc jockey and longtime Allen companion, "and I could tell that Tim was starting to salivate." During the initial days of the Detroit comedy scene, as Coulier told *Detroit Monthly*, he and Allen would "talk about (TV). That was something that we all sat and drank coffee till five in the morning and dreamed about." By the early eighties, only Coulier was close to making it more than just talk.

If Hollywood was going to be his destiny, he wasn't going to get there overnight, and he knew it. He continued to concentrate on his stand-up routine while searching for other ways to make money in Motown.

One way was doing commercials. Despite the slump of the early eighties, Detroit still reigned as the automotive capital of the world, and, as such, the Big Three and their subsidiary industries were always interested in a new friendly face to sell their products

to the public. Why couldn't that new face be
Tim Allen's? As Thomas Pagel, his instructor
from Western had observed a decade earlier,
Tim possessed that intangible quality which
endeared him before the camera, and the camera never lies.

Moreover, work in commercials or industrial films offered Tim the possibility of more
money than he could hope to earn anywhere
else at that stage of his career. A good national spot might be worth thousands. In contrast, most headliners at the Comedy Castle
and other clubs didn't normally pocket more
than $1,200 or $1,500 a week, while opening
acts netted much less. Comedy was no gold
mine.

Tim couldn't enter the corporate world
alone. He needed someone on the inside to
help him. He needed Eric Head.

It was Eric Head who had suggested to Tim
he ought to try stand-up comedy back in the
late seventies, and it was in letters to Eric
Head that Tim, writing from his cell in Minnesota, had shared his fantasies for the future.
They had talked about big offices with private secretaries.

The future was now. Tim Allen and Eric
Head had a chance to prove it was more than
just a fantasy.

As the supervisor of a Detroit advertising
agency, Head used his influence to put Tim
in spots for the popular Big Boy restaurant
chain, and for Action Auto, a franchise of gas
stations based in Flint.

"Big Boy wanted a kind of charming by-play between this couple, a James Garner–Mariette Hartley type of thing, and I put Tim in that." Head didn't doubt Tim's natural performing abilities, though he had to be extremely careful with how he pitched his friend.

"I wouldn't dare tell my boss that I was about to put a guy who had just gotten out of prison in a series of six or seven commercials representing our biggest account," Head said. "I purposely kept that confidential. When you're trying to sell a client on a spokesperson, you don't lead off with, 'He just got out of the slammer.' So Tim and I kept that to ourselves." With good reason, it seems. (Years later, according to *TV Guide*, "after hearing of his federal conviction for selling cocaine, advertising firms had yanked two national TV commercials starring Allen.")

Over the eighties, Tim appeared in dozens of commericals for a wide assortment of products, including Tuffy Mufflers, Michigan National Bank, Pella Windows, and K mart. It was never his first love, but it was a damn good day job. "They supported me through the first part of my career," he told the *Detroit Free Press* in 1990. "I was able to be not so concerned about money on the road because I had another job to help me out."

Tim and Eric Head also formed their own production company. At first, it was called DH Productions, a division of HeadDick Limited. Later, after they changed the name to

Boxing Cat, Tim got the notion of making a baseball jacket with the company's logo. "He bugged me forever," Head said, "to get one of these made, and I said, 'Tim, it's $170. I don't need that, and we really don't do anything in our company except a radio spot now and then. It's just a fantasy.' But he thought that if we had jackets, we would be a legitimate company."

For a short time after prison, Tim kept his job at the Sportsman, although he was becoming increasingly distracted by his other pursuits. "I don't know how many times I told him to get off the phone and get on the floor and get to work," recalled Charles Wilson III. "He's a mover and shaker, and was trying to make things happen for himself."

Eventually, he quit. The job that had been so useful in the days after his arrest no longer served a purpose. Damage control was part of Tim Dick's past, not Tim Allen's future. He also thought he could make the same money doing something he enjoyed a lot more than selling backpacks. "I just left," he told the *Free Press*. "By then, Ridley was paying $25 to the featured acts, and I figured if I could get four of those, it would be as much as the $110 I was making" at the Sportsman.

Tim left his job at the advertising agency, as well. He would still try out for commercials—they paid good money and presented the possibility of good contacts—but any other work was simply not worth the time it took away from his first love.

Tim Allen, for all his cockiness, for all the credit he received from Ridley and the comics, knew he still had plenty of work to do on his craft.

He was a long way from Johnny Carson.

11

For one thing, Tim was one of the dirtiest comics in Detroit. A significant percentage of his material was considered "blue"—the comics' inside jargon for profane, vulgar humor. That reputation had accompanied Tim ever since his early days at the Castle in 1979, and his first performances after prison didn't do anything to change that.

He may have looked innocent enough with his distinguished wardrobe and disarming mannerisms, but this was no choirboy. His act, from start to finish, was rated "R," filled with a barrage of sexual and scatological references. "It was like turning your guitar up real loud," Tim would say in later interviews.

He didn't know how to turn down the volume, or, if he did know, he didn't think it was necessary. He didn't just push the envelope; he pummeled it.

"He did a bit about how fathers teach their

sons how to urinate," Hayes recalled. "Most guys would just go through the moves. Tim actually said, 'You're there with your dad, you're proud, and then he whips out the big thing.' He goes for that little shock."

Jason Vines, who opened for Tim at Bea's Comedy Kitchen in downtown Detroit, said the headliner years later told him not to tell fart jokes. "I'm thinking that maybe he's giving me some advice," Vines said, "but it turned out he was doing a lot of fart jokes in his routine, and that's why he didn't want me to do them."

Yet, precisely because of how he packaged himself as a pure professional, Tim was the only comic who could get away with a steady diet of blue material. "It would be like your priest talking to you about sex education," recalled one comedian.

He had recognized his niche, had refined it, and was now going to run with it.

But how far could it really take him? Blue may have been suitable for the clubs, the traditional setting for the brashest, most uncensored form of comedy.

But blue would never put him on Carson. His bathroom humor would not go over too well in the living room. "For a long time, he was killing show after show," Tim Lilly recalled, "but everyone was looking at him going, 'What are we going to do with this guy? We can't put him on TV.'"

Tim was fully aware of the problem, though he didn't seem too inclined to do much about it. His comedy, he told the *Kala-*

mazoo Gazette in the mid-eighties, "tends to be a little risqué at times, a little bit blue. It's not sexual material, but it's sensitive. I get the job done whether it's using expletives or getting rude about the Russians with a very peculiar twist.

"I'm not a TV comedian. I have auditioned four times for 'The Tonight Show,' and twice for (David) Letterman. Nothing against them, but they like their favorites. You have to fit a format."

Tim was never the kind of comic to fit a format. He had his own format, and, better yet, he had Eric Head.

Head became Tim's writing partner and unofficial coach. He was not easy to satisfy, which is exactly what a raw, undisciplined talent like Tim required.

"He was very funny," Head recalled, but "he was rough and unpolished. He had no segues, and he had bits with no endings." They got together a few times each week to work on new material, although a lot of times, Head said, their sessions turned out to be "about two hours of writing and six hours of fart jokes and watching videotapes of movies we thought were funny."

But when Head did get serious, he suggested a few adjustments to Tim's act. "I'd write payoffs for bits that I didn't think had strong enough endings," he said. "I would type up stuff, send it to him, and he'd try it out. If I wasn't there, he'd make notes and say, 'this didn't work,' or 'this got a big laugh,' or 'this isn't my personality.'"

The student didn't always listen to the coach. On occasion, Head dispensed large bits in Tim's routine that somehow would "miraculously appear on stage the next night—just crude, nothing lines. Early on, he was doing just the worst stuff, lines like, 'You ever see a dog take a shit? It's like they really put their back into it. They make a circle first, and then they look at you for approval, like they picked the right area to take a crap in.' "

Tim's association with Eric Head made him a better comic, but it also made him a target again for some of his peers. "Most of us were really envious that he was in a position where he could do that," said Lilly. Added Jerry Elliott: "He had somebody writing for him, and we're working for gas money. Although we were getting the stage time and the experience, it was the writing that everybody had trouble with. Something funny and original was a necessity, and Eric was pumping it out."

Word even got around that Tim was paying for the material, which Eric Head, to this day, strongly denies. "Tim couldn't really afford it," he said, although he does add, "I did work one deal with Tim. He sold me his restored 1969 Volkswagen for $1,500, and on top of that, he said, 'Well, I really wanted $1,800, but make up the other $300 in comedy material.' "

His hard work was beginning to pay off. Within about a year of his release from Sandstone, Ridley started to regularly feature him as the club's headliner. Tim was also receiving prominent stage time at other regional venues, including the Holly Hotel.

His appearances at Bea's Comedy Kitchen, in a sense, epitomized the new Tim Allen, the one who had gone from sheltered suburbanite to cultured sophisticate. Bea's was a black club in a part of town that most of the white comics preferred to avoid. Not Tim. He even developed a small following there. "Tim was not afraid of us," said Tony Hayes, who is black. The audience was "used to a Pryor or Redd Foxx style, and then you have this white guy coming in there with a two hundred dollar suit on, and he was not uncomfortable. He had his opinion and didn't care what color you were."

Tim, according to a few comics, briefly put his prison experiences into his act, but soon realized that audiences wouldn't buy the fact that this well-groomed, clean-shaven, boyish-looking Midwesterner had spent any time in the slammer. An ex-accountant? Maybe. An ex-convict? Absolutely not.

Besides, he didn't want to be known as the comic who went to prison. He was trying to forget about prison. "He came up with some really funny material," Lilly recalled, "and I was trying to encourage him to do it, but he didn't pursue it with the hunger I've seen him pursue other new bits. He felt very uncomfortable."

He did, according to Hayes, feel comfortable enough to put his late father into his routine. Hayes said that Tim poked fun at the fact that he was told at the funeral parlor that the man in the casket looked just like his father. "Tim goes, 'That don't look like my dad,' " Hayes said. " 'That looks like a dead guy.' "

Whatever the subject matter, Tim was popular among the club owners. Comics were hardly the most consistent of entertainers, but Tim could be relied upon to put on a good show, and a good show meant a good crowd, and a good crowd meant a good profit. "I could maybe count the number of times on one hand over the years when he had a bad set," Mark Ridley said.

Detroit, however, was only one town, with only a limited number of top-notch clubs. Like it had been for so many of the well-known comics over the years, from Berle to Bruce, Lewis to Letterman, Martin to Martin, it came time for Tim to do the one thing, short of gaining national television exposure, that cements a coast-to-coast reputation.

It was time for Tim to hit the road.

He had to prove that he could generate applause outside of Michigan, outside of its Midwestern sensibilities, outside of its loyal crowds eager to cheer on their triumphant native son. He had to prove he was a national comedian.

He would have plenty of opportunities. The comedy epidemic was catching on all across the county. When Ridley opened his club in 1979, there were fewer than ten similar establishments in the whole United States. Now, there were dozens. "People had lost a lot of their strident attitudes, had become more accepting of life's dilemmas, and were looking for some kind of escapist entertainment. Comedy was it," said John Fox, publisher of *Just For Laughs* magazine.

To accommodate the rising demand, the comedy marketplace was soon flooded with thousands of new comics. Breaking out of that endless, almost-indistinguishable, pack would not be easy, and Tim, for all his confidence and creativity, couldn't be certain he had the right stuff to become one of the fortunate few to make it big.

"He used to say to me, 'Think I should just give up and go into the ad business?'" said Rick Bach, his high school friend and former advertising boss.

Bach, who owned Pacifico's, a bar in downtown Detroit, said that in the mid-80s Tim would often stop by to seek advice about his future. "In my opinion, he was close to just chucking the whole comedy thing," Bach added. "If he could've gotten a job in advertising, he probably would have done that." Bach said Tim, who had grown tired of spending so many nights on the road, asked Bach to find out if his brother-in-law, an ad executive, could give him a job.

At times, Tim, according to some of his friends, became frustrated by the fact that, even though he was doing well at the clubs and in commercials, he still needed to be financially supported by Laura, who was earning a very good living as a sales design representative for Planterra, an interior landscape company in Detroit. (Tim and Laura had been married in April of 1984 in Saginaw. The woman who had stood by Tim during his most desperate days would now stand by him forever.)

"He was grateful to have a woman like that," recalled comedian Lowell Sanders, who opened for Tim on numerous road gigs. "But it's one of those male things. He always wanted to be the breadwinner, and not put the pressure on her." Added Eric Head: "I remember a few remarks about him feeling a little bit like a loser cause Laura had a regular job. He used to say, 'I'm sitting at home with my socks on.'"

On another occasion, while vacationing in Mackinac Island, Tim turned to Rob Cowin, a close friend from Seaholm: "Am I ever gonna make any money?"

It was a very good question. Tim had already played a lot of good rooms, but things weren't moving fast enough for an ambitious talent who was still trying to make up for lost time.

In the mid-eighties, several times a year, Tim flew out to the West Coast to look for commercial and stand-up opportunities. He was fortunate to land an agent at a very reputable firm—Commercials Unlimited—but he didn't land much else.

"He sat and watched TV a lot," recalled Kim Flagg, the younger sister of his old high school classmate Scott Flagg, who had died in a drowning accident in 1983. Flagg, who became one of Tim's best friends in L.A., put him up at her apartment for weeks at a time.

"He had that remote going and going, waiting for someone to call, an agent or anything," she said.

But the phone didn't ring often enough, prompting Tim to joke he might have to take a "swan dive off the balcony," Flagg recalled. Tim had "moved up quicky into the ranks of the comedy world," as he told the *Los Angeles Times* in 1992, but "I was nothing special."

Tim, however, was not about to give up, and his friends were not about to let him. Hang in there, they kept urging him. Something good is going to happen, and it will happen soon, and when it does, the possibilities will be limitless. Tim didn't need much convincing. He was no fool.

"I could make $5 million a year doing comedy," Tim once told the *Detroit Free Press*. "That's what I tell my wife. Nothing has the same potential."

12

It was just another stop on the road for the weary comic, another town to conquer, another crowd to charm, another check to cash.

This time, the town was Akron, Ohio, home of the Goodyear Tire and Rubber Company, and not much else. The evening started out as another professional, yet routine, performance for Tim Allen, and it ended up as one of the most important nights of his life.

The salesmen in the crowd weren't buying his schtick. He was on his way to bombing. He had to come up with other schtick, and he didn't have much time.

"As I was dying up there," he told *Ladies' Home Journal*, "I was thinking, Tim, what you need is something these guys can relate to, and I thought tires, cars, tools. I love cars and I figured these guys must love them, too. So I just started naming tools, and as I did that, I growled like my brothers and I used to do when we sat around the dinner table waiting to eat. The salesmen laughed because they understood how simple men's needs really are, and it all came together."

It sure did.

"These guys loved it," Allen told the *Los Angeles Times*. "They started hooting and hollering. The more I talked about it, the more these guys responded."

In 1984, on one unexpected night in Akron, Ohio, of all places, Tim Allen had accidentally stumbled upon a new niche, and this one was far superior to the old one. This one would eventually earn him a ticket to Hollywood.

"He had created a testosterone-laded universe," the *Times* wrote years later, "in which his idea of heaven is visiting the tool section at Sears and his ultimate ambition is to rewire everything from the garbage disposal to the blender."

Tim has never tried to declare himself a comic genius for discovering the macho/tool angle. "It was new," he told the *Times*, "and it was so obvious. It was sitting right there . . . It took somebody, No. 1, who was really interested in it."

It also took somebody who could visualize its potential in the marketplace, and Tim never had any trouble doing that. He understood his audience in Akron, and he knew America was full of Akrons. Men are the same everywhere. His message was unmistakable: Men are pigs, and aren't we lucky? (It was most fitting that Tim would call men pigs, and that it would become his trademark. In Kalamazoo, he had a pet pig named Bacon.)

His new niche didn't turn him into an immediate superstar, but it did, for the first time, put him on the right path. He had been sorely lacking a distinct point of view, and now he had a very distinct one. He became the guy who talked about men's stuff. "I don't think it made his act any better or stronger," Tim Lilly said, but "it was an incredible hook."

The act didn't come together all at once. "The grunting part of it, the 'Men Are Pigs' part of it, and the tool time were three complete different ideas that meshed together into one character," Lilly added. "I saw him when he began to talk about tools but wasn't grunting. I saw him grunt and not talk about tools. The big joke in town was that if there was another orifice in the body that oozes something out of it, Tim Allen would have ten more minutes of material."

Comedian Diane Ford liked Tim's new niche, and encouraged him to stick with it. "He had done it once," said Ford, who often accompanied Tim on the road, "and I told him to grunt after everything he said. I thought the whole audience would be doing it after a while, and, sure enough, they did." Ford perfectly complemented Tim's act. "She'd talk about antimale and women type issues," said Chris Di Petta, who managed the Punchline in Atlanta, "and Tim would go up and speak his mind. It was pretty much a toss-up. Diane's pretty opinionated in her own right. She doesn't back off from anybody."

Eric Head, his writing partner, said Tim's

evolution on stage represented a natural pro-
gression for a comic who had grown frustrated with bits that didn't match his
intelligence. "As he developed more stage
time, and became more popular," Head said,
"he wanted to do material that had a little
more meat and substance. It wasn't just dirty
little observations. It became important for
him not to go up and talk about dogs taking
a crap." Or, as comedian Bruce Baum put it:
"The material caught up to his appearance."

One person, however, who was cautious
about the new hook was Mark Ridley, the
club owner who gave Tim his start in comedy. Ridley, five years after opening the Castle, wasn't about to make any guarantees
about anything. Nobody could be a fortune-
teller in this crazy business. "It was a good
callback," Ridley said, "but at the time, there
were so many people who had hooks, you
couldn't tell who was going to stand out."

But Tim Allen was not just another comic
who stumbled upon a new callback. Besides
enormous talent, he possessed an inexhaust-
ible work ethic and a gift for self-promotion
sorely lacking in many of his peers. Early in
his career, he had recognized that giving a
good performance onstage wasn't going to be
enough to make it to the next level. A comic
also had to give a good performance *off* the
stage.

"He's what I call a turbo schmoozer," Head
said. "Some guys can engage in a light kib-
bitz. He can go right to the full-blown power
turbo schmooze." For example, even though

they were the best of friends, Tim routinely wrote a formal thank-you letter every time Head put him in a commercial.

"There are a lot of guys who want to work hard and are incredibly funny," said Di Petta, "but don't have a clue about business at all, and there are other guys who really aren't that funny, but really know business and know how to promote themselves. Tim had both." Added Jerry Elliott: "I'd go to my dad's office and Xerox copies of bios and stuff and throw them in a manilla envelope with a bad 8-by-10 that my buddy shot in his basement in front of a sheet that we hung, and Tim had professional 8-by-10 glossies."

Head, in fact, used to constantly needle Tim about his obsession with marketing himself. "He was always coming in with a new press kit," Head recalled. "What happened to the one you had last month?" Head asked him. "Oh, I changed that to add a new review of a show," Tim responded. "Every two months, he'd have new head shots," Head added. "Comics are sitting at Denny's, and he's at the printer, getting his 8-by-10s."

Tim may have even been better at promoting himself in person. Tim and Tony Hayes were in Chicago once getting ready to appear in a comedy special when they spotted Budd Friedman, owner of the famous Improv club in Los Angeles. Tim asked Hayes to introduce him to Friedman. "He was always the guy who'd go, 'You know this guy? Can I talk to this guy?'" Hayes said. "A lot of guys rag on him, 'Oh, Tim, you're just kissing up,' but it worked for him."

Tim also believed in the power of the media. "A lot of comedians wouldn't want to do their act on the air and they only did the show because it was in the contract with the promoter," said his good friend Detroit disc jockey Ken Calvert, but Tim never complained. He was always grateful to get any exposure.

Once, in fact, according to Tony Hayes, Tim even made an appearance on a second-rate local dance show that featured an all-black audience. "A lot of the white comics said, 'Tim, why did you do that awful show?' And he goes, 'Look, man, it's TV,' " Hayes said.

Tim was an expert at working a crowd, and not just from the stage. He resembled a grass roots politician campaigning for votes, which, in a way, was precisely who he was—only he was running for fame, not office. "He was the guy who used to stand outside the comedy club and shake everybody's hand as they left," Head said. "He fell in love with the idea of people shaking his hand. He was the single most focused guy I have ever met."

Perhaps that's because comedy is a very serious business to Tim Allen. "He was a comedian that most of the other comedians looked up to," Jason Vines said. "He wasn't a dork, sitting around and always cracking jokes. He didn't have to be on all the time."

Tim seemed almost to take it personally when others didn't show the same respect toward his profession. "I remember showing up at the Castle for a 'Star Search' audition with twenty other comics," Leo Dufour recalled, "and I was wearing jeans and a T-shirt. Tim kind of looked at me and said, 'You've got to get with the program.' "

Self-promotion didn't mean a thing, of course, without the talent to back it up. All the splashiest 8-by-10s in the world wouldn't land him five seconds with Johnny Carson. "The bottom line was that he still had to drive to the gig and work," Elliott said.

No problem. Tim possessed the raw talent, and, maybe, just as important, he realized that he could never take that raw talent for granted.

Either he'd become a lot better or he'd remain a club comic the rest of his life. Once again, the future, as Judge McCauley had told him, was up to him. Once again, Tim made the right choice. He got better.

He was the first of the Detroit comics to videotape his stand-up performances. When Hayes asked him about it once, Tim told him it was because he wanted to study every move that he made. "He'd study every movement of his hand, every gesture," Hayes said, "and he'd have professional people come in to do it." Soon a lot of comics were taping themselves.

He approached comedy as an intellectual art form that should be carefully scrutinized. "Tim was the kind of guy," Hayes said, "who, if he found a good book about comedy, would tell the other comics to read it."

Tim also appointed himself, according to

Hayes, as the group's unofficial comedy advisor. "He'd tell guys how to do their acts, how to clean this up, or change that," he said. "I was one of the guys who never had endings, and he'd go, 'Tony, you got to put endings on this bit.'"

Like most comedians, Tim was willing to take his act anywhere. He told the *Detroit Free Press* he once worked a Holiday Inn during a Detroit Tigers playoff game in the early eighties: "Seven people are in this bar, the Tigers are winning, and I'm standing next to the seven-foot screen with the game turned up loud," Allen said. "I'm telling my joke . . . and I hear this, 'Shhhhh.'"

Another time he served as the emcee for Sexy Flexy, a male stripper. In his book, he wrote about how he was literally attacked by an army of horny women after Sexy had done his thing at a Michigan club.

He even played a suburban shopping center. "When he told me he was going to do it," Hayes said, "I said, 'You're crazy.' But that's how he sold himself. It was just amazing."

Tim had more than charm and creativity. Tim had chutzpah.

For instance, one night while performing at the Punchline in Atlanta, according to Hayes, Tim was given the middle act. The Punchline was one of the better clubs in the country, and the ever-ambitious Tim wasn't content with the number two position. He rarely was. Even though he was supposed to perform for only twenty minutes, he wound up doing thirty-five.

"He blew the audience away," Hayes recalled. "Whoever the headliner was that night couldn't follow him. The club owner came over to Tim that night, and goes, 'The rule of thumb is that middle acts never do that to a headliner.' "

Forget the rule of thumb. Tim, according to Hayes, learned another rule that night. Tim was given a lecture, but he was also given a promotion. The next time, he would be the headliner. Translation: You didn't have to win over the other comics. You had to win over the crowd, and Tim was a master at winning over crowds.

Once, later in the decade, Tim was on his way to play at Chap's Comedy Shoppe in Kalamazoo. The club usually put comics up at the hotel next door, but, Tim, as a first-class comic, according to Hayes, was no longer going to tolerate second-class treatment. "He said he was tired of staying in these dinky rooms, and asked for a suite," Hayes said. "We told him he wasn't going to get it, but he got it. This was a comic on the road, and he was staying in two hundred dollar suites. I knew then."

Others knew, too. When a *Detroit Free Press* reporter went in the summer of 1985 to track down the local comic with the best chance of becoming famous within the next five years, the trail led to only one prospect. "Tim was definitely Mark Ridley's guy," said the *Free*

Press's Laura Berman, "and Mark basically was comedy in Detroit."

Berman spent an entire week with Tim, and came away extremely impressed. "He was completely focused," Berman recalled. "He had this quiet confidence. It wasn't like arrogance. It was a very professional attitude."

The story was the first major newspaper piece ever written about him, and it was very complimentary. Wrote Berman: "Taking a repertoire of funny faces and voices, a practiced sense of timing and an ability to seem like a nice guy even while speaking the unspeakable, he's joined a handful of comics able to earn a living making people laugh."

Tim appeared to be completely open with Berman. He let her into his place of work—the Comedy Castle—and into his home. The only thing he didn't let her into was his past.

The story made no mention of Tim's troubles with the law, and there was a very simple explanation: Tim didn't tell her.

When Berman was puzzled by the large chunks of unaccounted time, Tim insisted that nothing important had happened to him during those years. But, Berman said, "I had been a reporter long enough to know that when people are covering stuff up, you can sense it somehow, and I said, 'Tim, if you're hiding something from me, I'm going to find out,' but he said there really wasn't anything."

Berman still wasn't convinced. She approached Ridley and a few of the local comics looking for some answers to the mysterious time gap, but they wouldn't give them to her.

Maybe some of them were jealous, even resentful, of Tim and his success. But, as a group, they were also very protective of him. They were not about to share his big secret to probing outsiders, especially members of the Fourth Estate. Over the years, in fact, as an entire new generation of young comics started to perform in Detroit, many would, eventually, pose the same question: "Did Tim ever go to jail for selling drugs?" "We all knew, but we never said anything," said Hayes. "That was our buddy."

The story received excellent play on the cover of the newspaper's Sunday magazine section, but soon after it appeared, Berman received the news she had dreaded. It was from someone who did know the big secret about Tim Allen. Almost immediately, she angrily confronted the evasive comedian.

"I was pissed off. It makes you feel you didn't do your job properly," she said. "He said, 'I'm sorry, but I didn't see how I could tell you. It would change the whole story. And I'm working real hard. I've done my time.'"

In a way, Berman could hardly blame the guy. If Tim had, indeed, revealed everything about his drug-related past, he was absolutely right. It definitely would have changed the context of the whole story. It would have turned it into a piece about a comic who had conquered prison instead of a comic who was conquering Detroit. He really didn't have a choice.

Tim, after all, was still on parole. "We used to have to call his parole officer to check in and let them know that Tim was working, and that everything was okay," recalled Chris Di Petta, who managed the Punchline.

In the mid-80s, word got around that Steve Hagerman, another Seaholm grad, was implicated in an international drug operation. Tim knew Hagerman from high school, and had even, in the early eighties, written radio spots for a big warehouse sports store that he operated in Birmingham.

When the "shit hit the fan," as Rick Bach, his former advertising boss put it, Tim was very worried that, because of his own past drug connections and cooperation with authorities, some people might conclude that he was still working for the government and had fingered Hagerman, which was not the case.

Finally, in 1986, Tim ended his parole. He was on the phone with Kirkland Teeple, owner of the Main Street Comedy Showcase in Ann Arbor, making plans for future club appearances, when there was a knock at his door. When Tim got back on the phone, he almost shouted into the receiver. "I've just been notified that I have completed my parole obligations to the government," he told Teeple.

For the first time in almost eight years, Tim had nothing to do with the law. He could now focus all his attention on his livelihood.

Tim Dick was more confident than ever that he would make Tim Allen a household name.

"Someday I will do something very funny on TV and film," he once told the *Kalamazoo Gazette*.

Junior Field Day chairman Tim Dick speaks to his class.

Courtesy of Seaholm High School

Tim and the cast of "Home Improvement" at the People's Choice Awards in 1993.

Copyright © Tao Kingman, Archive Photos/
Fotos International. Courtesy of Archive Photos

Tim Allen and his wife, Laura.

Tim plays golf with friend Ken Calvert.

Tim shows off his trophy at the Golden Globe Awards.

Tim hams it up at the 21st Annual People's Choice Awards at Universal Studios, California. *Copyright © Archive Photos/Lee*

13

As the eighties wore on, that day seemed to be getting closer and closer. The years of paying the dues were finally paying him the dividends. The friends who had urged him to be patient when he was discouraged had been right all along. "He was one of the biggest regional acts," recalled John Fox, publisher of *Just For Laughs* magazine. "Every region had its own individual that was the most popular, and Tim was Mr. Detroit."

He had the right mentality, the right message—and the right manager. Her name was Elaine Steffek, and she was Tim's biggest booster, perhaps just as important in the early stages of Tim's career as Mark Ridley and Eric Head. Steffek did everything for Tim, from attending all his performances to sending out tapes to schmoozing whoever needed to be schmoozed—even a turbo schmoozer needed a sidekick.

"The big thing with Elaine was that she got

him into the nicer clubs in the Midwest," said Chic Perrin, owner of the Indianapolis Comedy Connection in Indiana. "She did great on press releases, and she had a big part early on with the structure of his act, getting him to be more disciplined and serious about it."

Steffek managed him offstage, as well. "He liked to hang out and have a few cocktails," Perrin added, "and she really kept him on the straight and narrow. Tim used to say, 'If it weren't for Elaine, I never would have gotten anything going.'"

Soon, Tim became known as more than Mr. Detroit. He was playing clubs from coast to coast—the Comedy Works in his native Denver, Giggles in Sarasota, the Tropicana in Atlantic City. He was, according to the Kalamazoo *Gazette*, opening for well-known entertainers, such as the Spinners, Suzanne Sommers, and Jay Leno.

Tim hit the road two or three weeks every month, and he was very grateful for the work.

At times, though, Laura, according to Holly Hotel owner George Kutlenios, wasn't too thrilled with her husband's hectic traveling schedule. "She would always tell me about the travails that he was having on the road," Kutlenios recalled. "She wanted him to come home to chill out for a little bit. If he were single, he would have probably killed himself on the road."

Tim had two managers—Elaine Steffek and Laura Deibel. Where Tim was timid, Laura was tough. Where Tim was ambivalent, Laura was absolute.

"She's always been there to protect him from everything that's out there to get a piece of him," Kutlenios added. "Tim was a well-known commodity, and even in those days, you had people who liked to glom onto comics on a local level, and Laura always kept him away from that bullshit."

Tim certainly attracted his share of admirers, who, according to Tony Hayes, the comics referred to as "jokies" instead of groupies. "They'd come in, hang out at the clubs, and try to pick up comics, especially on Fridays and Saturdays," recalled Tony Hayes, though Tim, he said, showed the same allegiance to Laura as she had always shown to him.

Over the years, in a number of cities, Tim even developed a cultlike following. Fans flocked to the clubs wearing tool belts and pig masks. His grunts served as a mantra for the misunderstood man, the one longing to reassert his long-repressed masculinity against the rising force of feminism. Men, for a chance, could be men without apologizing for it.

They had formed their own new movement, and Tim was their de facto commander. "The guys pulled for his bit," friend Ken Calvert recalled. "He kind of defended us." As Allen once told the *Los Angeles Times:* "Women get mad, gays get mad and blacks get mad (when the jokes are on them), but men as a rule don't seem to care that we make fun of them."

Conversely, Tim's humor appealed just as much to the opposite sex. He was telling women things about their men that they had known all along, and he was giving them a safe place to unload their frustration. Men are uncouth. Men are liars. Men are pigs, and, yet, despite all that, we still love them. He was a marriage therapist with a microphone.

With both men and women on his side, it was no surprise that he became one of the hottest club comics in the country. He was also making a great investment for the future. "He would play Davenport, Iowa, Pittsburgh, a lot of the Southeast, the Carolinas," said comedian Jim McLean, "so that when his television pilot came on, the people in Greensboro, North Carolina, or Jackson, Mississippi, said, 'Hey, this is that Tim Allen about the tools thing,' and they would tune right in."

His popularity on the circuit also enabled him to defy the conventional wisdom in the business that a comic must be based either in Los Angeles or New York in order to be successful. He was deeply rooted in the Motor City, and, ambitious or not, he was not about to become another disloyal native son to skip town. "If you're not getting exposure, you have to move to L.A. or New York," said comedian Bruce Baum, "but Tim was getting exposure."

Besides, for all of Tim's growing appeal throughout the rest of America, Detroit was still his headquarters. Detroit was where he had started his stand-up career, and where he had received the most support. Detroit was also where he got his first big break.

In the mid-eighties, if a comic couldn't land on Carson or Letterman, the next best thing was cable. If one could book a few minutes on cable, it actually meant something, unlike today, where the endless lineup of comedy programs has sharply diluted their entire value.

The Showtime network, one of cable's pioneers, made comedy one of its main priorities. Without the regular built-in restrictions of traditional commercial television, Showtime could present comedy in its most outrageous and uncompromising form by going right to its source—the clubs. The network went from city to city—even to Alaska—in search of the best in local talent. In 1988, it stopped in Detroit.

Mark Ridley, despite the rise of other new clubs over the years, was still the ringmaster of comedy in Detroit, and, as such, the Comedy Castle was the natural choice to host Showtime's spotlight on Motor City comics.

In a sense, it was Ridley's unofficial coronation, a tacit acknowledgment of the man who had built the scene from nothing in the late seventies and early eighties. Naturally, then, because they were staging the party at his house, he felt it was only fair that he would have a say over who was on the invitation list. "If you're going to go to a club in a city, you should highlight the comedians who work there," Ridley said.

But, to guarantee a better show, network producers decided it would be safer to go for more-established talent instead of gambling on the locals. A national audience wouldn't show much tolerance for subpar performers.

Showtime won that battle. Ridley might have been the ringmaster of comedy in Detroit, but in Hollywood, he wasn't part of the circus.

He did win one skirmish, though, by persuading Showtime to put Tim Allen on the special. Showtime was not disappointed. "Other comics performed that night," Eric Head said, "but no one had the material or the charisma or the reaction that Tim had." Added comedian Jim McLean: "He put everybody to shame. There was no denying that it was his night."

It was the first of many nights for Tim Allen on Showtime. With that performance, he earned a trip to participate in the network's Comedy Club All-Stars event in Lake Tahoe, which showcased some of the best stand-up comedians from across the country. Once again, he put everybody to shame.

"I remember coming into the office on the following Monday," recalled John Fox of *Just For Laughs,* based in San Francisco, "and tracking down his representative, saying we really wanted to get him out here, and quoting the rate of pay that we were willing to pay for a first-time headliner."

The offer wasn't good enough. Tim, by that point, according to Fox, was "making such good money" at his regular stops in the Midwest and Southeast, that it didn't make any sense for him to "sacrifice $3,000 a week in order to expose himself to Reno, Nevada. He couldn't afford to expand."

Perhaps he wouldn't make the financial sacrifice for Reno, Nevada, but he would for Los Angeles, California. Tim, even if he preferred to retain Detroit as his home base, was fully aware that he would never achieve his ultimate goals unless he got some exposure either in Hollywood or New York. Johnny Carson wasn't going to send someone to scout Tim at the Comedy Castle in Detroit or the Punchline in Atlanta. Elaine Steffek knew it, as well, and sent videotapes of Tim to clubs in Southern California.

One tape landed in the hands of Bob Fisher, owner of the Ice House in Pasadena, who had heard about Tim from a club owner in Houston. Fisher took one look at this unknown comic from Michigan, and that was enough.

"Out of every hundred tapes, we find maybe three people who we would consider headliners here," Fisher said. "I think the Ice House is the hardest club for a comedian to get a booking at in the country. The only thing I remember about his tape was that it was a rare feeling that here was someone who was really good."

The Ice House, like many places in Los Angeles, paid less than other clubs across the country, but it was an important coup for Tim Allen. The club offered a tremendous history—Bob Newhart, Lily Tomlin, and the Smothers Brothers recorded their first albums there, and David Letterman, Garry Shandling, and countless others played it long before they became celebrities. The original contracts from Letterman and Shandling still hang on the club's wall, testimony to the humble origins of a comic's career, and to the limitless potential for worldwide fame.

The club also offered a tremendous location. Just a few minutes down the Ventura Freeway from "beautiful, downtown Burbank," which served as the headquarters for

the National Broadcasting Corporation—and
Mr. Johnny Carson—the Ice House belonged
in the regular rotation of comedy clubs fre-
quented by the right people, the agents and
producers and casting directors who turn the
anonymous into household names.

This time in Los Angeles, Tim wouldn't
joke about taking a swan dive off the balcony.
He wouldn't be flipping channels waiting for
the phone to ring.

This time, Tim had a chance to be discovered.

Which is exactly what happened, although
it wasn't an agent or a producer or a casting
director who made the first big discovery of
Tim Allen. It wasn't Steven Spielberg or
Aaron Spelling or Mel Brooks. It was Geno
Michellini.

Geno Who? Geno Michellini, a Los Angeles
disc jockey who, in 1985, had invented the
impossible, a way to make Angelenos laugh
during the most unbearable part of their lives:
rush hour.

Every afternoon, shortly after five, Michellini broadcast "The Five O'Clock Funnies," a
seven-minute reprieve from freeway hell,
which introduced hysterical bits from comics
scheduled to appear at local clubs. "It was
therapy," said Michellini, "so you could take
your mind off that asshole that cut you off at
five miles an hour."

Names such as Jerry Seinfeld, Sam Kinison,
Paul Reiser, George Wallace, and Dennis
Wolfberg got a plug on "The Funnies" before
doing a local gig.

Michellini didn't pay the comics, and he didn't have to. Everyone got something out of the deal. "The comics got exposure to over two million people in the biggest market in the country for what they did, including casting agents, producers, and directors," Michellini said. "I got material that nobody else in the country could get, and the club got asses to put in the seats." All Michellini required was the comic's permission, which was usually no problem.

Michellini had never heard of Tim Allen until he turned on television one night. Tim was on Showtime, and Michellini was in stitches. "Everybody in my house was falling on the floor laughing," he said. "He was doing his tool time routine, and he was hilarious."

A week later, Michellini asked the Ice House's Bob Fisher about Tim Allen. "He goes, 'Oh, yeah, he's a killer on the club circuit,' " Michellini said, " 'and, as a matter of fact, he is going to be here Tuesday night.' "

So was Michellini, and what he saw in Tim's set that night in early 1989 easily confirmed his original assessment of this unknown's talent. He had to book Tim on "The Funnies."

"Geno Michellini pushed the hell out of him," said Chris Di Petta.

Michellini introduced himself to Tim that night, and told him about his plans. Tim had no objection. Why should he? There wasn't any other way he was going to get that kind of exposure in a market the size of Los Angeles.

After securing Tim's permission, Michellini selected seven minutes from his Ice House routine. He put the material on the air a few nights later, and had no reason to expect much more than the usual dozen or so calls from approving listeners.

It's fair to say the public response was a little more enthusiastic than the usual. "In twenty-four hours," Michellini said, "the station got over five hundred calls. At that point, Tim had never been on Carson or Letterman, but people were going crazy. 'Who is this guy?'"

Jim McCawley knew about this guy. It was his job to keep track of the hottest new talent on the club circuit. His boss wanted to know these things. His boss was Johnny Carson.

Word spread that McCawley was scheduled to catch Tim's act at Igby's in Los Angeles. At last, almost twenty years after he told Pete Shelley in homeroom at Seaholm High, Tim Allen was close to making his prediction come true. Maybe, instead of staring at a Carson poster in the green room of a Michigan comedy club, Tim Allen would soon be in the most famous green room in America. Maybe it was destiny.

If so, destiny would have to be delayed. McCawley went to see Tim that night and thought he had some definite talent. But McCawley felt Tim Allen was not right for Johnny Carson.

According to Michellini, Tim had understood before his performance that night that McCawley considered him too dirty for late-night television, for the Middle America that expected wholesome entertainment before it went to bed. And, even though his material was no longer quite as blue as it had been in the early part of the decade, Tim was still Tim. He loved to get dirty.

But Tim was also still the superb salesman. If Jim McCawley wanted a clean act, well, then, that's exactly what Jim McCawley was going to get. The King of Comedy was dying to sit next to the king of late-night television.

Only one problem. McCawley arrived too late to see it. "Tim had done the equivalent of four six-minute sets of clean material," Michellini said, "to show McCawley that he could be clean, but McCawley showed up a half hour late, just as Tim was doing his regular stuff. He heard one swear word, and walked back out again."

McCawley, however, said it wasn't Tim's profanity that kept him from making an appearance on "The Tonight Show." He believed that Tim needed more time.

"Sometimes, I knew the material wasn't going to fly as well as it would if I waited longer, and, with Tim, that's what I did," he said. "It was always the most important shot of their lives when they went on with Johnny Carson. They had everything to lose by going on before they were ready and nothing to lose by waiting longer. They might not do well. He might not think they were terrific. He might not want them back right away. It could be detrimental.''

McCawley, who had booked hundreds of comedians over the years, was probably right, although the impatient Tim didn't see it that way.

All he understood was that his longtime dream of appearing on Carson would remain, at least for the near future, just that, a dream. ''When Tim found out,'' Michellini added, ''he was very frustrated. He couldn't get on any of the major shows. He couldn't get the exposure that his peers were getting.''

But while Tim may have been wrong for Johnny Carson, he was right for another legend in American comedy, Rodney Dangerfield.

Dangerfield had sent his staff to look for comics across the country to appear in his upcoming HBO comedy special. It wasn't the major networks, but it was still TV, and Rodney Dangerfield was still the big time.

The two made a perfect match from the start. ''He was just the kind of comic that Rodney liked,'' said Chris Di Petta, who represented another comic on the special, which was taped at the Tropicana Hotel in Las Vegas. ''He knew Tim's story, about the drug bust and all that. He liked people who were off base a little bit. He knew he was a real person.''

The affection was mutual. ''Tim was like in his pocket, following him around constantly the whole time,'' Di Petta recalled. ''He was very taken by Rodney. It was funny to watch.

Tim took a video camera with him, and documented everything."

The show itself—"Opening Night at Rodney's Place"—which aired in the spring of 1989, wasn't one of comedy's most memorable evenings, according to Di Petta. "It was really tough to look at," he said. "Dangerfield had definitely done better specials. It got so dirty later on that I think people actually turned it off." But not before Tim took his turn on stage, and, as usual, took over the room. "That was a big thing for him to do Rodney," recalled one comedian. "He used to go back and forth to New York to try to get on."

For Di Petta, it wasn't Tim's act that stood out from the Dangerfield special. It was his attitude.

Di Petta had known Tim since the early eighties, but on that night in Las Vegas he saw a different Tim Allen. He saw a comic who, perhaps for the first time, had become fully aware of his new status in the comedy community. "I can remember Tim saying, 'I guess it's our shot,' " Di Petta said.

As the decade drew to a close, it sure was Tim Allen's shot, and he made the most of it.

Even ultratrendy Southern California, as manifested by its overwhelming response to his material on "The Five O'Clock Funnies" and his subsequent club dates, embraced this unknown from the Midwest. "I never would have thought Southern California would have taken to me," he confessed to the *Los Angeles Times*. He was especially popular in conserva-

tive Orange County, which he attributed to
the suburban mentality, in which "taking care
of your house and going to the hardware
store are very fulfilling."

In Orange County, Tim played his first big
auditorium, the twenty-five-hundred-seat Celebrity Theatre in Anaheim. Michellini and his
partners, prompted by the success of "The
Funnies," decided to hold a concert there with
the show's most popular performers. Tim was
an obvious choice, although at first, Michellini
said, he considered the whole concept a bit
strange. "He wondered, 'I'm doing a concert
for a deejay?' "

Tim, of course, was doing a concert for
more than Geno Michellini. The Celebrity
Theatre, just like the Ice House in Pasadena,
was accessible to the right people. It was also
the biggest crowd of his life, and he didn't let
them down.

"He had barely taken the stage when many
in the audience started uttering his trademark
pig snort," according to the *Los Angeles Times.*
"At this rate, it may not be long before Tim
Allen becomes a household name."

It wasn't the first journalist to forecast fame
for Tim Allen, and it wouldn't be the last. The
fans had fallen for Tim, and so had the press.
The industry was next.

14

In the late eighties, Tim had to make another change in his act. This one had nothing
to do with his material, and everything to do
with his manager.

Elaine Steffek was Tim Allen's Moses. She
had delivered him to the Promised Land—
California—watching him steadily develop
from a raw talent to a polished performer. She
helped him with his act, both on and off the
stage, and along with Tim's wife Laura and
perhaps Eric Head and Mark Ridley, she had
been the person most responsible for his success. "She got him to the point where he
could go to the next level," said Detroit comic
Tony Hayes. "She was great on the phone,
great on getting things set up, great on getting
him auditions."

But could Elaine Steffek join him on that
next level? Did she have the contacts to take
advantage of Tim's rising popularity? And, if
she was able to track down the right people,

would she know how to make the best deals for her client? Most stars in Hollywood, after all, are like comets: They emerge suddenly from out of nowhere and disappear just as rapidly. The wrong deal, the wrong meeting, the wrong missed opportunity and Tim could remain a club comic forever.

Indianapolis comedy club owner Chic Perrin had once brought up those very concerns to Tim, but at that time the stubborn comic wouldn't entertain any possibility of dismissing his manager.

"He did nothing but rave about her," Perrin said, "although he was a little leery that she could take him to the next level." Tim, if nothing else, just like Laura, was extremely loyal. He was not about to dump someone such as Steffek, who had stood by him through all the ups and downs of the club circuit. Or was he?

After one trip to California, it became clear to Tim, according to Perrin, that Elaine Steffek was not the manager for the future.

"They went into meetings," Perrin said, "and I think Tim was convinced that based upon those meetings, she just couldn't deal with these people. He realized that she had Midwestern values, and when you go to L.A., it's pretty dog-eat-dog out there, and she just wasn't equipped to handle it. She thought she could, and he didn't think so."

Nonetheless, Tim was torn about what to do with Steffek, according to Kirkland Teeple, a club owner in Michigan. "He would agonize over difficult decisions," Teeple said, "especially when his career started to take off. He was enormously fond of Elaine. He was aware that this would be a very difficult problem for her because she was very committed to trying to help his career."

Ultimately, Tim chose ambition over loyalty. He wanted to seize his opportunity before it was seized from him, perhaps for good.

"He told me he was being handled by these people in L.A.," Perrin said, "and I asked him what happened to Elaine. He just said she couldn't take him. He wouldn't really talk about it much after that, because I tried to discuss it with him, but he was really just upset. What I understand is that they had a big blowup of some sort, because she obviously thought she could handle it. Tim just told me, 'It wasn't pretty, and we're not talking.' "

Just like that, it was all over. In the end, Elaine Steffek did suffer the same fate as Moses. She could take Tim to the Promised Land, but she couldn't stay there with him.

Tim's dumping Steffek did not go over too well with some of the Detroit comics, who were, in any case, always looking for a way to find fault with Tim. He was going places, and they were going nowhere. "I think the guys felt that she had taken him to a point," one comic said, "and that maybe she should have gotten some of the rewards. She got nothing."

Added another friend: "I felt bad for her. Tim didn't think that this sweet person in Lansing, Michigan, was going to get him on the 'Tonight Show.' She got him to where he was just one show away from his own sitcom, and she was gone."

Even Chic Perrin, who agreed with Tim's decision, didn't approve of the way his friend dismissed Steffek. "No question he did the right thing," Perrin said, "but he could've handled it better," implying that Tim even felt guilty about how he ended things. Perrin suggests Tim should have, at the very least, paid Steffek off.

In any case, Tim made the right move for his career. As comedian Lowell Sanders put it: "If he had stayed with her there, he'd probably still be there." Steffek, for all her admirable devotion to Tim's career, was based in the boonies. She maintained ties to club owners throughout the Midwest, but she didn't play ball in the majors, and that's where a major talent like Tim Allen belonged.

Understandably, according to comics and club owners, Steffek was devastated by the breakup. She had found a rare bumper crop, and now it had been taken away from her. "She was onto something," Perrin said. "She knew what he was capable of. She had more confidence in his ability than she thought he did." To her credit, he said, Steffek has never bad-mouthed Tim. "She just said, 'That's the way it goes. Tim's a great talent, and I think he'll do great.' "

Years after their separation, Steffek still won't discuss her long association with Allen, though according to Chic Perrin their relationship shows signs of warming up again. "Last time I saw her," he said, "I asked if she ever heard from Tim, and she said he sent her a really nice Christmas card. That was the first she had heard from him."

Steffek, to be sure, retains a vested interest in keeping silent about her early years with Tim Allen. She still works in the management business, and, as Perrin put it, "Maybe she'll get a comic somewhere down the line and Tim will help her. Why burn the bridge any further?"

Tim turned his career over to Richard Baker and Rick Messina. They did live in the right town and they did know the right people. Together they represented Tim's first professional team.

"These guys knew what they were doing," said Doug Pullen, a reporter for the *Kalamazoo Gazette*. "They were taking Tim through a very careful, methodical process to get him where they thought he could go. Baker was more the conceptualist, and had the TV know-how. Messina was more the day-to-day, get your fingers dirty kind of guy, like a road manager."

The key was to convince Hollywood to take a good look at their new client. It was gratifying to receive recognition from people like Bob Fisher and Geno Michellini, but Bob Fisher and Geno Michellini weren't going to make Tim famous and rich. He needed to attract serious interest from someone much higher up in the showbiz world. He needed to be discovered—again.

In the meantime, Tim kept doing what he

did best—stand-up comedy—and he was
doing it better than just about anybody. In
1989, he was selected as one of the five nom-
inees for the Male Comedy Club Stand-Up
Comic of the Year by the American Comedy
Awards. His competition included such
highly regarded talents as Jeff Foxworthy,
Richard Jenni, and Dennis Wolfberg.

Exactly ten years after he first stepped onto
the stage at the Comedy Castle in suburban
Detroit as an unknown, undisciplined comic
on borrowed time, Tim Allen had climbed to
near the top of his profession. He had
changed his life, and then changed his act.
There wasn't much else left to change.

"I'm where I always wanted to be as a
comic," he told the *Kalamazoo Gazette* in early
1990. "People are looking for me. I'm not on
too high a level, but a nice level. I have room
to move up, and a lot of room to go down.
I'm paying my bills and now people are hearing about me."

Tim was happy to be nominated, but of
course he wanted to win every competition
he entered, whether it was a drag race on
Woodward Avenue or the American Comedy
Awards. According to his good friend, Ken
Calvert, Tim was far from content when the
award was given to Foxworthy. "I think Tim
thought he was going to get it," Calvert said,
"and when he didn't win, he was really disappointed. He was more than a shoe salesman
with fifteen minutes; he had a genuine act.
First things first, he wanted to be the best
stand-up comedian out there."

Yet he wasn't so sure that he wanted all the trappings that went along with success. He treasured his privacy, and even back then, when he was still an anonymous club comic, he was already afraid of losing it. "The next step of celebrityness is one I don't really want to take," he told the *Gazette*. "I have friends in the business who want that, but it's not something I care about. I was not an insecure child."

Moreover, Allen now had a family to protect. He had a new daughter, Kady, who changed him forever. "It was the biggest thing in his life," said Calvert. "I remember the day the baby was born. He needed to sit down. He was absolutely speechless. It took a couple of days for it to sink in."

Tim has stated publicly that he and Laura didn't want children, that they didn't believe they would be good parents. "The lunatics inside both my wife and me were still scared, and maybe a bit selfish," he wrote in his book. "What would I do with a kid? What would a kid do with me?"

What changed his thinking, he said, was the time he observed the special bond between a close friend and her father. He saw them embrace, and knew instantly it was something he wanted to experience, and he's never regretted it. "It's the best thing that ever happened to us," he wrote.

Tim also had a past to protect. He'd been extremely fortunate to keep it hidden from the press so far, and he saw no reason to change that strategy. He knew if the whole

truth came out about Tim Dick, it might jeop-
ardize everything that Tim Allen had worked
so hard for over the last nine years.

In early 1990, when the *Gazette* started
printing numerous articles about the local college boy who made good, there was no mention of his drug problems or his prison
sentence, although, like Laura Berman five
years earlier, reporter Doug Pullen knew
there was something missing in the Tim Allen
story. "Tim would imply that there had been
some skeleton in his past," Pullen said, "but
he danced around it. I don't think he was trying to be deceptive. He was protective, and it
was understandable."

Pullen tried to check up on Allen's past
with the university, but it showed no refer-
ence to any Tim Allen in its archives. Pullen
didn't know at that time that the comedian's
real last name was Dick. For now, Tim Allen
could dance around his past, and get away
with it. He was still a club comic.

Not for much longer, though. Even if it
meant sacrificing his privacy, Tim was determined to reach his potential. After all, how
many times could he play the Punchline in
Atlanta or the Indianapolis Comedy Connection in Indiana? "He had gone just about as
far as he could go with the stand-up side of
his career," Pullen said. "If he had just stayed
in that, he was going to get burned out, and
at age forty-five, he might have to open up a
tool shop."

15

Tim Allen would never have to open up a tool shop—at least not in real life. By 1990 he was reportedly earning more than $50,000 a year on the club circuit, with a strong following in cities all across the nation. A Tim Allen concert had become a major event. "When Tim was introduced, he used to walk out with Peter Gabriel's 'Shock the Monkey,'" recalled comedian Brent Cushman, who opened for him at the State Theater in Kalamazoo in February of 1990. "Nobody could step on him. He was just seventeen feet tall on stage."

As the *Gazette* put it, his comedy featured "an affectionate skewering of the modern family and a lewd look at the not-so-vicious war between the sexes.

"Punctuating his bits with caveman grunts . . . Allen sketched a world filled with men and women who get along just fine, but they don't understand each other. Men lie and engage in one-upmanship, particularly as it applies to hardware, while women ... take two hours to pluck out their eyebrows and 'one hour to draw them back in.' "

His management team moved quickly to capitalize on Tim's momentum, and one of their targets was Dennis Johnson, Showtime's vice president of original programming. Showtime was a major player on the cable comedy scene, and Tim had already appeared on the network.

For Baker and Messina, the trick was to persuade Johnson to see their client perform live. As talented as he might seem on tape, nothing could quite recapture the genuine excitement of seeing Tim Allen in the flesh. Baker phoned Johnson periodically to rave about Allen, but the Showtime executive was very busy. He often heard agents and managers raving about their clients, and didn't have time to see everyone.

Baker, however, according to Johnson, was careful not to cross that thin line between persistence and pushiness, once again confirming how wise Tim had been to get rid of Elaine Steffek. Richard Baker knew exactly how to play in the major leagues. "He is an extremely low-key and a very gentle man in this crazy business," Johnson said, "and because he's very intelligent," he wouldn't promote someone unless he strongly believed in him.

One night, Johnson attended a party at a friend's house, and Richard Baker was also there. Lo and behold, the topic of Tim Allen came up. "He said, 'You really got to come see this guy,' " Johnson recalled. So, finally, Dennis Johnson went to catch Tim's act in person.

Normally when he checked out new talent, Johnson chose to play the dispassionate observer. He went to the clubs to make important business decisions. He didn't go to have a good time. "My response to stand-ups is not laughing," Johnson said, "but saying, 'This is funny,' or 'That is funny,' because I'm addressing myself to the structure of the joke, and how that story is being told, but not responding to it."

But when Johnson went to see Tim, the distant spectator gave way to the devoted fan. Tim Allen was discovered again. The last time, with Geno Michellini, it put him on the radio. This time, it would put him on the map.

"He made me laugh out loud," Johnson recalled. "He had really wonderful storytelling, and could create a situation that was very funny and relatable to the masses. You could be eight years old and laugh, and you could be eighty years old and laugh. I thought that was very unique, and different from most of the comics coming in at that time. I had not seen that kind of ability to tell those types of situations, based on true events, since Bill Cosby had come along."

Johnson was also impressed that Tim could weave together his tales of male-female relationships without resorting to shallow, vindictive attacks on the opposite sex. He was no Andrew Dice Clay. "A lot of comics were talking about women in a very negative manner," he said, but Tim's comedy "wasn't female bashing and it wasn't male bashing. It was really material based on truth."

Amazingly enough, Johnson also viewed Tim as "one of the cleanest acts that I had seen in a long time. He wasn't pushing that profanity envelope that a lot of guys push." Tim Allen had certainly come a long way since he was the blue comic from Motown who talked about bee vomit and farting.

Now it was up to Showtime to figure out where to take him next. All it needed to do was find the right vehicle, and Tim would take care of the rest.

Within a month, Johnson had inked a deal with Tim and his managers. The right vehicle for Tim would be his own prime-time special. "We made a decision very quickly on that," Johnson recalled. "He deserved his own special."

Showtime was also bright enough to let Tim be Tim. Instead of trying to mold his talent into some kind of preconceived image they had manufactured for him, the network set out from the start to present the comedian at his best, as the tool guy. There was no reason to mess with a formula which had obviously worked so well at concert venues across the nation. The only question left was where to host the special.

Baker and Messina reportedly leaned toward Los Angeles, probably because it was the logical place to capitalize on their widening industry connections; but Tim preferred to stage the concert back in his beloved Michigan. In L.A., it would be just another routine Hollywood special. In Michigan, it would be a major event. "In New York or Los Angeles, any person can see a lot of TV production," Johnson told the *Gazette*. "They can get so jaded by being so exposed to it."

By shooting it in Michigan, Tim would enjoy a huge home field advantage, and he needed every advantage he could get.

A special on such a prestigious cable channel as Showtime presented a tremendous opportunity—and a tremendous risk. If it became a hit, either critically or commercially, it could be perceived later as a major turning point in Tim's career, when he passed the threshold between club comic and rising star. Yet, if it failed in front of the critics and fans, Tim might never get such a great shot again. Nobody ever hears about the promising performers who don't match their expectations.

In Los Angeles, if he struggled, he wouldn't be able to count on much help. In Michigan, everyone would be pulling for him. He would be able to draw strength from his legion of fans, friends, and family members. It was a giant support system. "That's where he felt comfortable," Johnson said. "He was already so well known in that community. In that community, he always was a star."

Besides, as Richard Baker told the *Gazette*: "Tim's act is about being a Midwestern suburbanite, it's about those sensibilities. He's proud of it."

The most obvious Michigan location was

Mark Ridley's Comedy Castle, the site of Tim's stand-up debut in 1979. Forget about Geno Michellini and Dennis Johnson and Eric Head and Elaine Steffek, and even Laura Deibel. Without Ridley, Tim might still be selling backpacks and fishing rods to rugged Michiganders. "Mark saved Tim," said comedian Brent Cushman. "Mark was very important in giving Tim an awareness that he was going to be bigger than all his problems, that he had places to go if he wanted to."

But the Comedy Castle didn't have enough space for the kind of event that Showtime had in mind. Tim needed a much larger auditorium, a place which could generate a lot of noise, and show him off in the most flattering manner possible to the rest of the nation. He had to create a buzz, as they say in the industry, that could propel him to the next level of fame.

There was another obvious choice—the State Theater in Kalamazoo. Just a few months earlier, Tim had sold out the fifteen hundred-seat arena. "The only thing I knew about Kalamazoo was the Kellogg's in (nearby) Battle Creek," said Johnson. Nonetheless, Kalamazoo was going to be it.

Actually, in a way, Kalamazoo made the most sense for Tim's national coming-out party. After all, it was in Kalamazoo where Tim Dick had committed the biggest blunder of his life, where he had dealt drugs, disgraced his family, and doomed himself to more than a year behind bars. Afraid to check into the real world, he had hung around after graduating from college, and had turned into a big-time loser.

Now, more than a decade later, in the same town, in front of many of the same people, he had a chance to become a big-time winner.

16

Tim understood the moment and what it could mean to his career. Since that fateful evening years earlier in Akron, Ohio, when, in the midst of disaster, he discovered gold, Tim had carefully chiseled the rough edges off his masculinist message. He had matured, both as a performer, and as a man. He had been nominated as one of America's five best club comics. Finally, now, in the spring of 1990, he was ready for the next level—television.

But was national television ready for him? It was a very legitimate question. Just a year earlier, for instance, Jim McCawley hadn't been so sure, which is why he didn't book Tim on Carson. Granted, cable was no Carson—it didn't subscribe to the same limited boundaries—yet it was still, nonetheless, the small screen, which could not expect to provide the same energy and intimacy as a live performance at a comedy club.

Even Tim, on the eve of the network special, had some doubts. "They (Showtime)
showed some confidence in me that I don't
share," he told the *Kalamazoo Gazette*. "They
think I can do it."

They certainly did, and they were going to
do everything possible to prove it. The network brought in a thirty-member crew, six
cameras, a fifty-seven-foot video production
truck, and a custom-built set. Baker and Messina would produce the special, entitled "Tim
Allen Rewires America," and Ellen Brown, an
award-winning veteran of cable and network
television, would direct.

The team was set. Now it was up to the
talent.

As usual, the talent was terrified. "I'd never
seen a guy so nervous in my life," said his
close friend Ken Calvert, who served as the
evening's announcer. "He was digging a
trench. I think he knew that this was the one
that was going to bring it all together."

Terrified or not, the talent did not disap-
point. From the moment he seized the microphone until his final bow, Tim Allen used
Showtime to make it to the big time.

Everything went right—his delivery, his
timing, his facial expressions, his grunting—
and, as expected, he drew more and more energy from the wildly partisan crowd. Many
showed up with strap-on pig noses and
grunted their approval throughout the night.
The hometown boy was auditioning for
America, and they weren't going to let him
fail.

He gave two separate performances that
evening, allowing Brown a chance to choose
the best material from both. During the taping, however, she didn't have much to do.
"He was doing an act, and we were covering
the event," she said. "We just placed the cameras, and followed him. That was about it."

Even when things didn't go exactly as
planned—ironically, for the man who likes to
rewire every household appliance with more
power, a power failure interrupted the second
show—Tim, who doesn't like to ad-lib, knew
how to adjust.

"Am I having a stroke up here?" he joked.
"Sure, Galesburg and Plainwell are pitch-
black now," he said, referring to nearby com-
munities, "but I'll bet Upjohn's have all the
power they need." Said Pullen: "He just
started making shit up on the spot, and the
crowd was eating it up. He was hilarious. Afterwards, he said he was panicked when the
lights went out, but you couldn't really tell."

Tim returned over and over to his most
trusted topics—the male obsession for tools,
and the fundamental differences between the
two sexes.

He talked about how his "nipples get rock
hard" when he visits the Craftsman tool section at Sears, and how "men are lying shits.
We would lie about lying if we had to. Men
lie cause they're sick of women bitching at
them." A lot of the material was very familiar,
especially to Tim's diehard fans, but he made
it sound fresher than ever with a spirited performance. "Men are pigs, right women?" he

asked the crowd. "Just too bad we own everything."

On that night, Tim certainly owned Kalamazoo. As he walked off the stage, it was clear to many who worked on the special that Tim had passed another turning point in his career, and that there would be no going back. "He was soaking wet," Calvert recalled. "I was standing there, waiting for my cue, and I got the chills. It was obvious that the mission was accomplished. It was like, 'Tim, it's been nice knowing you.'"

The mission had only started. Tim had conquered the crowd, but he still had to conquer the critics. The *Gazette,* not surprisingly, raved about his show—"a thumbs-up for his painfully funny performance"—but the final verdict would have to wait till the show aired in the fall, when the reviews and ratings weighed in.

Meanwhile, Baker and Messina had plenty of work to do. Tim was still a club comic unknown to most of the important players in Hollywood.

A special on Showtime might give him more exposure and prestige, but there was still a tremendous gap between cable and the networks. For the third time, Tim needed to be discovered.

He was still a long way from his dreams. "A year from now, it's reasonable to assume that something will happen," he told the *Gazette.* "Either look for me in a development deal of some sort, or behind the counter at Arco. I think it's my mother's natural pessimism. There's a part of me that's as afraid of success as I am of failure."

Fortunately, Tim couldn't have picked a better time to make his move. His face was being circulated around town just as television executives were looking for the next Roseanne—the next anonymous comic to make the step from stand-up to stardom.

After all, Hollywood, for all its liberal pretensions, is a very conservative company town. If something in the industry works, producers don't try to always figure out why it works. They just keep doing the same thing over and over until it stops working.

But was Tim the new face they were looking for? Was this average Midwesterner really prime-time material or just another overrated club comedian? Sure, he knew how to tell a joke, but would he be able to act? Could he really be the next Roseanne?

"The thought of stardom appealed to his ego," said reporter Doug Pullen, "but I think the pragmatist in him wasn't quite so sure anybody was going to give a damn about him."

17

The pragmatist was wrong. There was one person who did give a damn about him. His name was Jeffrey Katzenberg.

Katzenberg was chief of Walt Disney Studios. One day, a few company executives were going over new projects when someone slipped a tape from one of Allen's stand-up performances into the VCR. "We were sitting in the room practically snoring," Katzenberg told *Time* magazine "He set the room on fire. It was like everyone had touched a raw electric wire."

A decision was quickly made that this Allen guy was worth a much closer look, and it wouldn't be from some wet-behind-the ears talent scout or assistant programming chief. This Allen guy would have to face the boss, Disney chairman Michael Eisner, and other top executives.

If Eisner adored him, he was set. If Eisner objected to him, he was sayonara. Allen seemed perfect for Disney. The studio had recently abandoned one-hour television dramas to focus on half-hour comedies.

The scene, appropriately enough, would be the famous Improv club, owned by Budd Friedman. A few years earlier, Tim, the turbo schmoozer, had bugged fellow comedian Tony Hayes to introduce him to Friedman, one of the most influential comedy club owners in the business. Now, on Friedman's stage, Tim would be going after a much bigger catch, one that could give him a lot more than some time at a comedy club.

Exactly a decade earlier, in a Minnesota prison, he had been auditioning for his life. This time, he would be auditioning for his fame.

He passed.

"He was just hysterically funny," recalled then vice president of comedy at Disney, Dean Valentine, who had some initial doubts as to whether Tim's "incredibly edgy and angry" stand-up routine "could be translated into a situation comedy."

Eisner, who reportedly showed up at the Improv wearing a Mickey Mouse sweatshirt, windbreaker, and sneakers, loved Tim's act, and afterward, greeted him with the good news: Disney wanted to have a meeting with Tim Allen. "Eisner is a man short on words," Tim told the *Los Angeles Times*. "After the performance, he said, 'Top to bottom, I liked it. You had a beginning, middle, and end, and you were succinct. I laughed all the way through the act. I liked the character. Congratulations.' "

Most performers would have been so over-whelmed with such flattery from a big Hollywood player like Michael Eisner that they would automatically agree to whatever the almighty Disney Corporation had in store for them. They were the experts, after all, who had been in the entertainment business for years, and obviously were much more attuned to what would sell to the American public than an unknown comic from Birmingham, Michigan.

But Tim Allen was not like most performers. He was not going to do anything that he didn't think was right for his career. He was fully aware that, for Disney, it was just another gamble on a promising newcomer, and if the gamble didn't pay off because they put him in the inappropriate role, so what? They could just pick the next promising newcomer.

But Tim would only be a promising newcomer for so long. If his first chance on network television bombed, he might never get another one. For every Roseanne there were dozens of others who failed when they tried to make the conversion from stand-up to prime-time. Tim had already seen that happen to fellow comedians such as Kevin Meaney ("Uncle Buck") and Lenny Clarke ("Lenny").

During the first meeting, when, according to the *Detroit Free Press*, Katzenberg said, "The Walt Disney Corporation would like a marriage with Tim Allen," the bold comic quickly

replied: "Tim Allen would like to see the ring
first." Perhaps he had acquired the courage
from surviving prison—or surviving the road,
or both. In any case, he stood up to one of
the most powerful corporations in the world.

Katzenberg offered Tim the starring role of
a New England schoolteacher in a sitcom version of the popular feature film *Dead Poets Society*. Thanks, but no thanks, Tim said. When
he told Tony Hayes about it, Hayes thought
his old friend had gone mad by turning down
a television series. "He goes, 'I'm not Robin
(Williams, who played the teacher in the
film). I'm Tim.' " He wasn't Tom Hanks, either, so he also rejected the studio's invitation
to star with a dog in a TV version of *Turner &
Hooch*. Disney was 0 for 2, and Tim was still
without any work.

After he received those offers, Tim was totally confused, later telling the *Los Angeles
Times*:

"I thought they got the wrong guy. I told
them, 'I'm the one you saw on stage doing
the men thing, grunting like a pig. Without
being disrespectful, wouldn't that seem like
an odd idea?' They weren't vehement. They
just said we could get you on the air with
that, and then maybe later ... It seemed like
they were preparing for failure the first time,
and then we'd move on to something else. I
think much to their surprise, as well as my
own, I said, 'I don't think I want to do this.'
And that didn't sit well with anybody."

Tim wasn't even sure he was doing the
right thing. As he later confided to the *Detroit*

News: "I wished I'd had a father figure, my dad or an older brother, somebody to tell me what to do."

Actually, Tim knew exactly what to do. If he was going to succeed in his network television debut, he would have to play the same character he had carefully crafted all those years on the club circuit. He already knew all the lines, all the voice inflections, all the mannerisms. He *was* that guy on stage.

But if he tried to become someone else, it probably wouldn't catch on. He was no Olivier, after all. He wasn't even a Stallone. He was a Tim Allen, a grunting male crusader with a message about men that he hoped to carry to the masses. If club audiences across the country were gravitating to his act, why couldn't television audiences do the same?

Yet, as much as Tim had always craved the spotlight, from Seaholm to Showtime, he was not obsessed about appearing on prime-time television, which actually worked in his favor. He could afford to wait for the project that interested him instead of settling for whatever came first. "I don't want to sell out to do a sitcom," he had said in an interview with the *Gazette* before taping his Showtime special. "I'm not Hollywood bound."

In a later interview, he told *Ladies' Home Journal:* "I'd finally reached the stage where I could work on weekends and spend the rest of my time with my wife and daughter. But I loved that character (the grunting tool man) and I wanted to see what it would be like to put him in a family situation."

If a domestic environment could work for Roseanne, it could work for Tim Allen. "If Disney can get him on the air and faithfully translate what's been exciting in the clubs the last couple of years into a good quality sitcom," Richard Baker told the *Gazette* in 1990, "he's got a chance of becoming a Roseanne Barr kind of phenomenon."

Finally, Disney came around. The comedian prevailed over the conglomerate.

Dean Valentine said Tim had support for his position all along from other executives in Disney. "Jeffrey (Katzenberg) tends not to put too fine a point on these kinds of things," Valentine said. "He makes a deal with a guy he thinks is funny, and he's got projects and he tries to stick one in with the other. He can sometimes be mechanically minded on creative issues." At the same time that Katzenberg was encouraging Tim to accept the other two sitcoms, which were in development at NBC, Valentine added, "many of us were whispering" to him to turn them down.

The tool man, however, was still a long way from taking his tools to the small screen. Television is a long, painstaking process, mined with as many obstacles as opportunities. Everything had to be in perfect harmony—the producers, the writers, the cast, the network. Any one ingredient out of sync, and the whole well-conceived plan to spring Tim Allen on America could easily fall apart.

"It's like a mutual addition," Allen told the *Gazette* before he went to Los Angeles to meet with Disney writers. "I've got to like them and they've got to like me. More important, they've just got to get (the concept right)." As a stand-up, Tim had been spoiled. He was used to absolute control over every part of his act. He was the scientist who had built the tool man, and he wasn't about to place him in someone else's hands unless he was certain they would know exactly what to do with him.

Once again, Tim was a man who understood the moment. "I'll never forget when he said, 'Something big is on, Charley. If it works, it's going to be unbelievable,' " said Charles Wilson III, his former boss at the Birmingham sporting goods store. "He just said, 'it involves Disney. I can't tell you any more than that.' He had an excitement in his voice and face that you don't see very often."

At the same time, Tim was wise not to take anything for granted. Even if he got along with Disney's writers and they were able to get the concept right, that still didn't guarantee Tim a slot on prime time. The show would first have to get approved for a script, then a pilot, and finally it would require an official go-ahead for a series production. He was still an unknown, and the ultracompetitive television networks, fighting for lucrative advertising dollars, might not be ready to take a chance on him just yet.

He went ahead with the rest of his career. The first stop was Montreal, Canada, the site of Just For Laughs: The Montreal International Comedy Festival, which would be broadcast on cable. It was another opportunity to show the people in the industry that he was one of the best stand-ups in America. "It was a real important showcase," recalled Chris Di Petta, who managed the Punchline in Atlanta. "Everybody in the industry was there at one time."

But Tim Allen wasn't the only one trying to gain a little exposure. So was a British comedian named Chris Lynam, who, as it turned out, gained more than just a little. Lynam ended his act by stripping completely naked and inserting a lighted Roman candle up his rear, singing "There's No Business Like Show Business." There certainly isn't.

The crowd went crazy, which was great for Lynam, but not so great for Tim Allen—he was the next act. Now Lynam had done to him what Tim had done to so many other performers over the years, and, as witty as he was, there was no way to follow that kind of shocking exhibition.

Tim started out by doing his standard routine, but quickly realized there was no point. The crowd was still buzzing about Lynam.

As a result, Tim did the only thing he could do. He deviated from the script, making impromptu jokes about what Lynam had just done. Just as he had ad-libbed when the power went out a few weeks earlier in Kalamazoo, Tim demonstrated how smoothly he could salvage an apparent no-win situation. He did so well at the festival that he later received an ACE Award for best performance in a cable comedy special, beating out Billy

Crystal. This time, he didn't have to say he was merely content to be nominated.

After Montreal, there was still the matter of the Showtime special, renamed "Tim Allen: Men Are Pigs." Originally slated to air in October, Showtime moved it up a month to get it out before the new network television shows made their debuts in late September. It would be much tougher then to get publicity for the star of a cable special.

Tim seemed satisfied with the final product. "The big thing now," he told the *Gazette*, "is to make sure the public hears about it and get people to see this thing."

The critics got to see it first, and they liked what they saw.

The *Detroit News*: "He's polished his material—heavily punctuated with Allen's trademark bestial grunts, yelps and snorts—into a flowing, half-hour routine that's more than ready for prime-time cable."

The Village Voice: "Allen avoids bland generalizations about what a man is and what a woman is. His monologues are detailed, personal."

The *Kalamazoo Gazette*: "In addition to being a solid, imaginative writer, he has mastered the physical side of his comedy. His use of varied facial expressions, gestures and body movements only add to the vivid imagery of his writing."

It was quite a way to start out the decade. Within just a few months, Tim was discovered by Showtime and Disney. His masculinist monologue, once confined to the comedy club, was now on the verge of entering the living room. Tim Allen, the ex-con, the ex–Tim Dick, the ex–lost soul, was on his way to Tinseltown.

18

Disney, once it had decided to go with the unproven Tim Allen, next needed to complement him with a proven producer, someone who could mold his raw promise into polished pay dirt.

If the wrong person were put at the helm, no matter how original the concept, how unique the talent, and how clever the script, the project could be doomed from the start. Besides his lack of experience in the medium, Tim was also an untested personality. Disney had to find someone with similar sensibilities to get along with this stand-up comedian from the Midwest. The chemistry had to be just right, or it would be wrong.

They briefly tried a couple of producers on the lot, but none of them clicked. Then, it was time to give Matt Williams a try. Williams, however, was very reluctant to work with another comedian.

It was nothing personal—Williams had

never even met Tim Allen. It's just that he
wasn't too thrilled about what had gone
down the last time he hooked up with a
stand-up trying to make the transition to television. Her name was Roseanne Barr, and it
turned out to be a nightmare. "He was very,
very nervous," Dean Valentine recalled. "Everybody told him that Tim was a really, really
good guy, and that he's a very different kind
of person than Roseanne. He was really
burned good by Roseanne, and I don't think
he was up for being burned a second time."

Williams lasted only thirteen episodes as
the creator of "Roseanne," before she used
her new clout to get rid of him. What guarantee was there that Tim, if he became just as
powerful, wouldn't turn out to be another
Roseanne? In any case, Williams didn't see
how he could come out of the whole thing
a winner.

"There's a double-edged sword that comes
with creating a series around a stand-up,"
Williams told the *Los Angeles Times*. "You're
damned if you do, damned if you don't. If
you take a stand-up and create a series
around them, and perfectly capture their persona, then you're accused of ripping off the
stand-up act. If you don't capture it perfectly,
and change it at all, then people say, 'Well,
those guys obviously can't write, because they
missed the whole essence of the stand-up.' At
the risk of sounding arrogant, when you think
about all the people who tried it, the success
rate really isn't that high."

Nonetheless, Williams, who had a three-year development deal with Disney, agreed to do lunch with Tim at the Garden Terrace, one of the cafeterias on the lot. Why not? He had seen him on tape, and thought he was very funny. Besides, perhaps Williams hoped that instead of Roseanne maybe Tim would more closely resemble another comedian he had worked with, Bill Cosby—Williams had been the head writer of "The Cosby Show," the television hit of the eighties.

It turned out to be a great first meeting. "They were actually making a connection at a deeper level than just, 'Hey, you're a funny guy,'" Valentine said. "They talked about going to church when they were kids. I think Tim was real happy about the lunch, and Matt was real happy about it, and Matt liked parts of (Tim's) idea a lot." Added Allen, in an interview with the *Detroit News*: "We started talking about the gist of the show and guy stuff, and really hit it off."

It made sense that they would get along so well. Both were roughly the same age, both had been raised in large families, both came from the same part of the country—Williams grew up in Evansville, Indiana—and both were very serious about their work. Tim was clearly not another Roseanne, and no matter how unlikely it was for a stand-up comic to become a star on the small screen, Williams was now more than willing to, at least, help Tim get his chance.

Williams was no fool, though. This time he took some steps to make sure he was prepared in case he later did encounter another

power-hungry star. Dean Valentine was right.
Matt Williams was not about to get burned a
second time. "Tim and I made it clear," Williams told the *Los Angeles Times*. "I am the
executive producer on 'Home Improvement.'"

Once authority was established, and the
whole team was in place—Williams was
joined by his partners, Carmen Finestra and
David McFazdean—the next move was to
come up with the best blueprint for the series.

Tim, of course, would play the lead character, and the show would explore some of the
themes he joked about in his stand-up routine. Beyond that, all sorts of details needed to
be worked out, and Tim was not timid about
suggesting his ideas for the series. He did,
after all, know the character better than anyone else.

"I pitched Matt a rough idea for a show
called 'Hammer Time' that would examine
the modern male point of view," he told the
Los Angeles Times, referring to his initial sug-
gestion for the sitcom. "But in that series you
would not have known if Tim Taylor (Allen's
character) was putting you on or not. He
would get pissy about women on his (do-it-
yourself) show and then he would go home
and be nice to his wife."

Tim also stressed the importance of making
the show as authentic as possible. One way
to accomplish that was basing the fictional
family in his home state of Michigan. Tim
suddenly had the kind of power even he
couldn't believe. "He was really surprised
that it wasn't a fight," recalled his good friend

comedian Lowell Sanders. "He figured these guys were going to be a real hard-nosed group, but he got in there, and they pretty much listened to what he had to say."

The premise was in place, and it was almost time to tape the pilot. But, first, Williams and his partners had to do something about the star. They had to teach him how to act.

On stage Tim was in complete control. He knew when to deliver his lines, when to grunt, when to show facial expressions, and when to wait for applause. He only had to play off one other element in the whole performance, the crowd, and he certainly knew how to do that.

But as an actor in a television series Tim would have to acquire a brand new range of skills. He'd have to show off other, more sensitive, layers of his personality and evolve from the cussing, vigilant defender of male territory to the responsible father of three boys. This was going to be a family show, not an extension of his "Men Are Pigs" concert tour. Perhaps most important of all, Tim would have to learn how to play off the other characters in the show. Acting is about dialogues, not monologues.

Tim knew he needed help in his new profession. "I was very nervous," he told *Ladies' Home Journal.* "Before 'Home Improvement,' the sum total of my acting experience was appearing in the background in a Mr. Goodwrench commercial." In a later interview with the magazine, he said: "I can only play a part if I can draw on personal experience, and that well can go dry pretty quickly."

He wasn't the only one who had some questions about his acting abilities. So did some of the Detroit comics. They knew him better than his new friends in Hollywood, and they knew he was no actor. "The consensus was that 'he's a great comedian but he can't act, and the show won't last,'" said one comic.

The comics were jealous, and who could blame them? One of their own was headed to yet another major accomplishment while they played the same old clubs in the same old towns in front of the same old faces. Some of them probably hoped that Tim would fail.

But Disney wasn't going to let that happen. Tim was dispatched to David Regal, an acting instructor at the University of Detroit. One of Regal's former students was actress Angelina Fiordellisi, who was married to Matt Williams. Regal knew Allen from the early days in Detroit, when both auditioned for commercials and industrial films. He would be able to do whatever it took to get Tim ready for his first television pilot.

Regal and Tim spent a few months reading Neil Simon scripts back and forth to each other, looking for two-people scenes that could teach the raw actor how to stay in character throughout a half-hour sitcom. "The stand-up experience he had was almost diametrically opposed to what an actor does," Regal said.

"The stand-up does his scene, which is

maybe three lines, and then, completely unlike the actor, either joins the audience in a
laugh or hopes he'll get the laugh ... as opposed to the actor, who maintains that wall
between him and the audience. All we really
did was stay consistent and hold for the
laugh, and not in any way betray to the audience that you think it's funny or that you are,
in fact, aware of their presence." Tim, according to Regal, made the transition "amazingly quick."

His pupil also benefited, he said, from the
experience of doing commercials and industrial films for years in Detroit, so that "when
he hit California, the camera and the sound
stage were second nature to him. The indus-
trials were no big risk for him. If you're really
terrible, nobody at Chrysler evaluates you,
puts it on paper, and lets the world know that
you stank in the training film for accessories
or parts."

Tim had something else going for him. He
had spent years in front of live audiences. He
would not be intimidated at television
tapings.

Over time, Tim, the comic, became more
confident of Tim, the actor. "I was able to get
by where I was working with professional
actors in California, and no one even said,
'Are you an actor?' " Allen later told the *Detroit News.* "It was amazing. I passed. I passed
that point where I thought maybe I'd look like
an idiot. Well, I plan on looking like an idiot,
that's part of the show. But intentionally."

The spring of 1991 was a wonderful time

in his life. The character he had first discovered on stage in Akron and had tinkered with from coast to coast for half a decade, stood an excellent chance of reaching the whole nation at one time. But Tim knew enough about the business to make sure he didn't celebrate too early.

"He was totally confident that everything he had to do with it was going to make it go forward and work," Regal said, but "he'd been up and down a few times, so he kept pretty much in control."

He again dedicated himself to a world he was sure about—stand-up comedy. Showtime, fresh off the success of "Men Are Pigs," asked Tim to do an encore. This one, entitled "Tim Allen Rewires America," would be filmed at the Power Center in Ann Arbor.

He also made a triumphant return to the State Theater in Kalamazoo. For Tim, Kalamazoo now stood as a reminder of his resurrection, no longer a symbol of his setbacks. He came back a bigger hero than ever. He also came back, according to the *Gazette*, with an awareness of what might lie ahead for him if his show did become a hit. Tim, the newspaper said, seemed to be "already planning ahead for when the supermarket tabloids begin scrutinizing every inch of his personal and professional lives ala Roseanne Barr."

Tim, at the time, could afford to make jokes about the issue. "Nobody believes I went to Western Michigan," he said. "They've never even sent me an alumni magazine. OK, so I've had three names and they can't find my records. I can see it now. A local Vanilla Ice." A few months later, Tim would not find anything amusing in the media search to uncover his past.

After his acting lessons, it was time for Tim to shoot his first television pilot. ABC, from the start, had been the obvious choice.

For one thing, Matt Williams had already created a blockbuster for them—"Roseanne"—and, despite the producer's heavily publicized run-in with the star, the network was very interested in any other projects he was doing. For another, ABC's head of development, Stu Bloomberg, enjoyed a good relationship with Disney's Dean Valentine. Finally, ABC thought Tim had talent.

Bloomberg came over to Disney, had a meeting with Williams, bought the basic premise of the show, and gave the official go-ahead for a script. Once the script was approved, it was time to shoot the pilot. Tim's costar would be Frances Fisher, a relatively obscure actress perhaps better known for the man she was dating—Clint Eastwood—than any work she had done.

Disney and ABC were very excited about the project despite the no-name cast. They had under contract a top talent in Allen, raw or not, and a top producer in Williams, who had a part in two of the biggest television shows of the last decade—"Cosby," and "Roseanne." Why not one more?

"There was so much excitement behind it from so many different levels," recalled Kim

Flagg, Tim's close friend, "that you couldn't help but feel that something was big."

Something was wrong, too. ABC soon realized that Fisher wasn't the right fit with Tim and the rhythm of the show. Flagg recalls greeting her stunned friend after he had just emerged from a meeting with the network brass. "He said, 'Everyone's excited. They think it's going to be great, and they just got rid of the wife.' It was real scary to him," she said.

No doubt it was scary to Tim. It was, after all, his first experience in the often unforgiving, high-stakes world of network television, where every performer is a hostage to the whims of executives in three-piece suits. He would also miss any chance of becoming best pals with Dirty Harry. Eastwood had come to see Tim do stand-up before the pilot, Flagg said, and "Tim was all giggly about it."

Added Dean Valentine: "Everything worked great on the show except for Frances Fisher. She was a terrific actress, and very believable, except she wasn't funny and there was no chemistry. It was just painfully obvious that she was holding up the show, and that we had to do something about it. There was a lot of resistance from the director, John Pasquin, who really believed in her. She just wasn't right for the part."

Fortunately, Disney had another actress on the lot to take her place. Her name was Patricia Richardson. "This all happened in the space of twelve hours," Valentine said. "She thought it was just going to be a short gig because she thought the show wasn't going to be going anywhere. She had just had twins, and she was a bit reluctant to go back to work. She wanted to nurse her babies . . . But it was immediate between her and Tim, an immediate chemistry, and it sent the show into the stratosphere.''

Valentine said Disney has produced other hit shows, but this was the only time "I actually felt it was going to be special right after the table reading of the pilot. It just clicked together, and you could feel it.''

Tim could feel it, too, but he remained cautious. A lot of shows start out with a good feeling—and end up with bad ratings.

But "Home Improvement" seemed to always have a guardian angel looking over it. During the show's planning stage, two new books about men soared toward the top of the best-seller list: Robert Bly's *Iron John: A Book About Men*, and Sam Keen's *Fire in the Belly*. Bly, an award-winning poet, became the spiritual leader of the revitalized "men's movement," whose members, fed up with feminism defining how they should behave, felt the urge to loudly proclaim their primitive masculinity.

If, perhaps more eloquent, it was nonetheless the same primal message that Tim Allen had been giving on stage for much of the eighties. On that night in Akron, Tim had first sensed that urge and had made it the cornerstone of his comedy. Now it would fit perfectly into his new sitcom, and Bly's book offered more evidence that there would be a big audience for it. "There is a part of me that wants to stand on a mountaintop naked and howl at the moon," Matt Williams told the *New York Times*. "I just thought I'm a crazy Midwestern maniac. Then you go, wait, other people feel this too? Really?"

Tim could also relate to what Bly was saying on a more personal level. "Mostly the book is about finding the father, a male mentor," he told the *Times*. "I missed, just as Bly said, the experience of standing with another man. Just standing there you absorb something of maleness."

The show, like any sitcom, needed to set up a conflict, and needed to settle that conflict in about twenty-two minutes. Once again, the literary world made a big contribution.

This time, it was Deborah Tannen's book, *You Just Don't Understand: Women and Men in Conversation*. It was Tannen's theory that men and women simply possess different communication skills, often making it difficult, if not impossible, to speak the same language.

Perfect. On "Home Improvement," Tim and Jill Taylor would get into all kinds of marital disputes because they don't speak the same language. The Taylors, after all, were no different than any family in America, and Tim Taylor was no different than any man. "He's a man who says, 'I'm a little confused; I don't know where the lines are anymore,' " Williams told the *Times*. " 'I don't know what I'm supposed to be anymore. I'm trying, damn it. I'm trying to be a good husband, a good father, but I keep screwing up.' I feel that. Tim feels that. A lot of guys in their thirties and forties feel that right now."

With help from Robert Bly and Deborah Tannen, "Home Improvement" was ready to establish its point of view and make its imprint on American pop culture. ABC, in fact, was so high on the show that it placed it in the most enviable time slot imaginable—the Tuesday night lead-in for top-rated "Roseanne." It was a very high compliment for an untested premise with an untested star.

Madison Avenue was a believer, as well. Advertisers singled out the show as the upcoming season's most promising new hit. Tim, however, didn't put too much stock in what they had to say. "I don't know who these people are," he told the *Detroit News* in the summer of 1991. "I don't know much about any of this stuff, but we've only done one show, for cryin' out loud."

Tim was a realist. "It (the show) could go one season, it could be a bomb, or who knows. It could be a missile and really take off . . . I have been a failure in my life so many times, so failing doesn't bother me." Added one friend: "I think he actually felt it was going to be more of an exposure thing. They were going to put two or three in a can, cancel the whole thing, but hopefully somebody would look at it and pick him up for something else."

But on occasion, especially in private, the realist in Tim gave way to the ego in him.

"I remember seeing him in L.A. I was there for some business," said Michael Souter, his old Seaholm classmate. "We went for a walk on La Brea, and this was before his first show, and he turned to me and said, 'You know, I'm going to be fucking famous. You watch and see.' And I did not believe him."

That summer, Tim attended his twentieth reunion at Seaholm High. He hung out with the same old gang, telling them about his upcoming television show. He showed a few of them some footage.

From Woodward to Hollywood, the class cutup had certainly come a long way. The emcee of Swingout was about to become the star of prime time. September—and a whole new life—was only a few months away.

19

First, however, ABC, Disney, and, most of all, Tim Allen had to deal with August, and it was one bad August.

From his release from Sandstone in 1981 till the eve of his commercial television debut—ten full years—Allen had managed to protect his past.

Only his family, his close friends, and the stable of Detroit comics from the early eighties knew he had been a drug dealer who did time. Everyone else saw him just as he wanted them to see him: A clean-cut, devoted professional from a large Midwestern family. Even the obscenities he spouted from the stage seemed out of character with his wholesome, congenial appearance. He looked like a guy who had sailed through life without even a parking ticket.

Tim had also kept Sandstone from the press. He had sensed, and rightfully so, that if the news leaked out, he would become

171

known as the comic who conquered cocaine instead of the comic who conquered the clubs.

It was a great angle, one that journalists would not be able to resist. In 1985, when the *Free Press*'s Laura Berman inquired about the large chunk of unaccounted time, and five years later, when the *Gazette*'s Doug Pullen snooped around Kalamazoo looking to solve the same mystery, Allen told them nothing. He stuck to the present and the future, and it worked.

But Tim was approaching a whole new level of fame. Club comics, even ones with their own cable specials, can escape close scrutiny. Audiences will laugh at their material and not wonder too much about the man behind the punch line. Fans, however, want to gobble up every bit of information they can about the private lives of their television stars. If they're going to allow them into the intimacy of their living rooms, they damn well want to know who they are, and the press is never shy about telling them.

It wasn't like Tim didn't expect it. A few months earlier, he had even joked about it with a reporter, suggesting that one day, people from Kalamazoo would rush up to him in the street questioning his college credentials: "Hey, he never went to Western! He's from Comstock!"

Even his friends got into the act. "When Disney was promoting the shit out of him," recalled comedian Tim Lilly, "I just sort of made a joke to Tim that, 'for $50,000, I don't have to go to the *National Enquirer* and tell them about you doing prison time.' And I wasn't the only one doing it. The other comics were teasing him."

Tim could laugh about it then—but in August it was no joke. That's because, just one month before Tim Allen, the new Roseanne, was to be unveiled to the American public, Tim Dick was forced out of hiding.

If it had been up to Tim, of course, Tim Dick might have stayed in hiding forever. But it wasn't up to him.

One of the tabloids, as the story goes, had started to make some inquiries about Tim's drug-related activities in Kalamazoo, and suddenly his whole future seemed in jeopardy.

He had a perfect right to wonder if, once the word got out, the American people would still accept him, Madison Avenue would still believe in him, and ABC and Disney would still stand up for him. Maybe he would be abandoned as abruptly as he had been adopted. Just ask Pee Wee Herman how quickly things can change.

"It was an extremely intense couple of weeks," his wife, Laura, told *People* magazine in 1992. "If we were Three Mile Island, we would have had a meltdown."

Disney, to be sure, wasn't about to take the news lightly, either. The company had invested a lot of time and money into Tim Allen, and had assumed, rightfully so, that it knew his whole story. It didn't. "Somebody at Disney came to the studio in a panic," Tim told the *Detroit News*, "and said, 'Is this true . . .

They actually overreacted, I think. They said, 'Why didn't you tell us this?' "

Tim said he just hadn't found the right time and strongly denied that he was trying to keep it a secret. "You can ask anybody in the comedy business, and they know it," Tim told the *News*. "It just wasn't common knowledge yet, because I haven't had time to talk to everybody."

In another interview, however, Tim didn't seem like he was about to make a confession to anyone, certainly not Disney or ABC. "I was hesitant to tell (the producer)," Allen told *TV Guide*. "I'd paid my time in prison."

In any case, it didn't matter that Tim hadn't told them before. The real issue was: What do we do about it now? They had to come up with a strategy to neutralize the potential fall-out as much as possible. If the story came out the wrong way, if the proper spin wasn't put on it, Tim could potentially lose credibility that he might never be able to regain, and "Home Improvement" could be headed for the bottom of the Nielsens. In television, image *is* everything.

They had two choices: Ignore the issue or tell the truth. Williams and Disney opted for the truth.

"I was a journalist for a long time," Disney's Dean Valentine said, "and trying to hide these things is always the worst thing because it always plays so much worse. It comes out as a revelation rather than when you're controlling the news. Tim was fearful, I wasn't. It just seemed like so long ago, and he had become such a devoted family guy. I had no question that, in the end, it would just make no difference. We never had any doubt that it would blow away."

Who could blame Tim for not wanting to tell his story? It was his life that was going under the microscope, not ABC's, not Disney's. He was the one who would have to live with it forever.

"When I told him that we ought to release the story, in a straightforward and truthful manner," Williams told *TV Guide*, "his knee-jerk reaction was, yes, we should tell the truth, but he didn't want his family dragged through the mud and hurt. I told him that, if he wanted to protect his family and minimize (adverse publicity), his best course was to be straight. Candor, honesty—those things are appreciated by everybody."

Strangely enough, it was even possible that Tim might emerge in a stronger position from the experience, a prime example of the unique modern star who is not afraid to come to terms with his past transgressions. America sometimes likes its heroes to be flawed—as long as they are honest about their flaws.

Tim reluctantly agreed to come forward. First, he needed to warn his family, and it wouldn't be easy. He had put them through so much a decade earlier, and now his past would all come back again, and this time it would be spread across a whole nation.

The family, as always, was totally supportive. They had stood by Tim during his darkest hour, developing the damage control strategies that mimimized his time in confinement, and helped him rehabilitate his reputation. They were, as Bill Bones had put it, ready to circle the wagons again. "The people we knew all knew it anyway," Bones said, "and accepted it a long time ago." As Tim told the *Detroit News:* "My mom and family said, 'You haven't had a lick of trouble since. What have we got to hide?' I said, 'Nothing.'"

Perhaps, but Tim was furious about it. He was approaching middle age, and didn't see one good reason why something that had happened almost fifteen years earlier in another life needed to be rehashed. "My personal thought was, it's no one's business . . . it has no relationship now," he told one publication. "I forced my brother to sit in a red ant pile at the age of three. What does that matter now?"

His contention, and it could certainly be justified, was that he had been a completely different person when he got in trouble. He was an aimless and angry young man, still mourning the death of his father. In any case, he had already taken responsibility for his indiscretions. He had never tried to blame anyone else, and he had done his time in prison. As Judge McCauley had suggested, he had taken his punishment like a man. Wasn't that good enough?

Maybe in Michigan, but not in Hollywood. Tim Allen had become a public figure, and now, like every other celebrity, he would have to appear before a new judge: the American people. Their verdict would likely decide his future in show business, and he wasn't about to predict the outcome. "You don't know what people are going to think," he told *TV Guide* a few months later. "I'm a pragmatist. I'm not the kind of person who celebrates before everything is in."

Nonetheless, he was confident he would receive fair treatment. "I trusted the American people to understand what had happened," he later told *Ladies' Home Journal*, "that I'd been a stupid kid, had learned my lesson and had gotten my life on the right track."

The national daily, *USA Today*, was the logical outlet for his confession. This way, he would reach the entire population in one broad mea culpa instead of allowing the story to fester by slowly building momentum across the country from one city to another. This way, it would be apparent that he was quite willing, from the beginning, to tell his secret, that he had nothing to hide.

The secret came out on August 16 in a cover story in the paper's Life section with the headline: *"Budding star owns up to a criminal past."*

It turned out to be an absolute masterpiece in public relations. It couldn't have worked out any better for Tim Allen if Disney or ABC had written it themselves.

The story revealed the sympathetic tale of a vulnerable family man who had taken responsibility for his actions, and who had wisely used prison to turn his life around. It didn't dig up any elaborate details about his transactions in Kalamazoo, the bad crowd he hung around with, or about how he had ratted on other dealers to make things better for himself. "Allen hopes that by talking about it now," the story said, "he can put the past behind him and prevent a scandal."

More importantly, it contained the well-rehearsed responses from ABC and Disney that demonstrated a united front, which they needed to keep Madison Avenue and Main Street on their side. The new television season was only a few weeks away.

"As far as we're concerned, this is something in Tim's past that he's taken care of," said Robert Iger, ABC Entertainment president. "It will not, in any way, diminish our enthusiasm for the show or for Tim Allen. We don't view it as a problem and don't think a big deal should be made out of it."

Williams was even more effusive: "To me, this is a success story. This is about a guy who got a second chance, and look at what he did with it."

He went on to say that even if he had been completely aware of Tim's drug activities before they started to work together on "Home Improvement," he still would have wanted to go ahead with the show.

It was done. Tim had finally told the whole truth about his other life, and now he awaited the verdict.

"A lot of people thought it was suicide" for him to go public, recalled George Kutlenios, the owner of the Holly Hotel. "But once he decided to let it go, I think it was cathartic. It was like someone had opened up a dam. Tim had finally put that (the past) behind him. It was always something that was his background that he had to get through."

That same day, the *Kalamazoo Gazette* carried excerpts of the *USA Today* article and soon other newspapers across the country followed.

But within a few days the story was dead. Allen even appeared on a national morning news show shortly after the confession, and there wasn't asked even one question about his months in prison. Nobody cared.

Tim Allen had survived the return of Tim Dick. By dictating when and how to release the truth, Allen and his damage control team had kept his credibility and career intact. They had defused a potential time bomb, and could now resume the important business of crowning a new star. The past was back where it belonged, and, this time, for good.

"What could they (the tabs) say about me?" Tim told *USA Today* a year later. "I did what I was supposed to do. It might have been different had they come up with it themselves."

20

September finally arrived. It was time to find out if the network and advertisers were right about Tim Allen. The critics thought so.

"Stand-up comic Tim Allen is a human drill boring a hole in usually impenetrable prime time," wrote the highly respected Howard Rosenberg of the *Los Angeles Times.* " 'Home Improvement' is that rare new comedy series that gives you a rush."

From the *Detroit News:* " 'Home Improvement' is the funniest and most imaginative new comedy of the fall season, bar none . . . If the Monday Night Football crowd hangs around ABC the following night, Allen is as sure a bet for national confirmation as Clarence Thomas."

The press was on his side, but what about the public?

Would his souped-up version of the modern maladjusted male really make an impact on the American psyche? Would women and children—the most traditional sitcom viewers—be able to relate to this testosterone-driven tool man? Would it give *them* a rush? Or would Tim Allen go down as another in a long procession of anonymous stand-up comics who couldn't make the leap to the small screen?

Matt Williams didn't have any doubts that Tim would be the exception. "I don't like to jinx anything," he told the *News*, "but this is a Top 10 show."

Williams didn't jinx a damn thing. By November, the show ranked ninth in the Nielsens, and had, as Madison Avenue predicted, clearly established itself as the fall season's biggest new hit. It captured its time period seven out of eight weeks, losing only to the World Series.

"It became pretty clear by the third or fourth episode," Valentine said, "that this show was just gaining tremendous momentum. People were watching it and talking about it. You could just feel the whole thing."

You certainly could. The country had instantly fallen in love with Tim Allen. Women went for him because he perfectly represented the well-intentioned, incompetent man. Men, who didn't normally tune in to sitcoms, liked Allen because he was clearly one of their own.

One writer summed up Tim's instant impact on the American household: "Finally, a guy can find something else on weeknight television besides Monday Night Football and the ESPN Sports Center. And to make good matters better, a fellow doesn't even have to fight the wife for control of the remote. She'll probably want to watch the show with him.''

From the beginning, Williams and the rest of the "Home Improvement" staff were able to preserve the essence of Allen's stand-up act, yet broaden it enough to make it appeal to Middle America. Williams had been wrong. He wasn't damned if he did, damned if he didn't. He had emerged as a winner.

Stories about Allen soon began to pop up in numerous newspapers and magazines everywhere. He was becoming the new sitcom superstar, the new Roseanne, though he seemed to go out of his way to separate himself from the old one.

"We're just so different," he told the *Los Angeles Times*. "I don't know that she did comedy as long as I did. Taking nothing away from her genius now, because she's brilliant, but I was on the road for so damn long. Plus I did commercials for years. So this whole thing hasn't intimidated me. And I think it might have frightened her a bit."

He may not have been intimidated by his new popularity, but there was one casualty of success that he wasn't crazy about—his privacy. Tim had often expressed fears that this might happen, even, at times, implying that he wasn't convinced the fame would be worth the loss of freedom.

With his face plastered across television sets from Maine to Montana, there were few safe places for him to hide out anymore, and that would be the case for some time. "I remember him mentioning about how taking his daughter for ice cream turned into an event," the *Gazette's* Pullen said, "and how people stopped by his house while he was mowing his lawn because they recognized him. He hated that."

Like most celebrities, because he suddenly had so many pressing demands—other people's livelihoods now depended on him—Tim couldn't keep the same regular contact with a lot of the old gang anymore.

"There was word on the street that Tim had forgotten a lot of people," George Kutlenios said, but "I don't think that's something that he can rationally choose on his own. Situations dictate that, not the person. How could he possibly have the same amount of time as he used to?"

Furthermore, Tim, despite his hectic schedule, was determined not to abandon his Michigan roots. He had always defended the Motor City, and he wasn't going to stop now that he had become famous. Even after he had inked the deal for "Home Improvement," he didn't make any immediate plans to move to Los Angeles.

"He was never crazy about the New York or L.A. lifestyle," Kutlenios added. "It wasn't something he wanted to immerse himself in. He had a lot of friends here. He had his family still around. It was a classic home boy situation. He was going to commute." Laura wasn't crazy about setting up a new life in La-La Land, either. She, too, had her friends and her family in the Midwest.

But once it became clear that the television series—and Tim Allen—would be an entertainment fixture for some time, it was obvious that Tim, Laura, and Kady needed a permanent residence in Los Angeles. He was no longer an unknown Detroit comic making a run at the big time. He *was* the big time, and the big time was in Hollywood, not Michigan. No matter how he might have once felt about L.A., he would now have to call it home.

Star or no star, there was one thing that Tim was not going to give up—his stand-up act. As good as he had become on television, Tim was far better on stage. He was better without censors and without sponsors. He was most at ease with that special energy that can only be generated at a comedy club, not a sound stage.

In November, Allen returned to the Celebrity Theatre in Anaheim. It was a nostalgic homecoming of sorts. At the same venue, two years—and a lifetime—earlier, he had made his first major public appearance in Los Angeles, thanks to the buzz generated from Geno Michellini and "The Five O'Clock Funnies." This time, the buzz was even louder. He was becoming, as he had told high school friend Michael Souter only a few months earlier, "fucking famous."

Nonetheless, he knew the wisdom of returning to his roots and polishing his craft. Doing stand-up was a chance to expand from the strict boundaries required by prime-time television. "It's my show," he told the *Times*. "I don't have to worry about writers, produc-

ers, or censors. They (audiences) get the full
bore ... It's a great release. And it's what got
me here."

That same month, Tim Allen took his stand-
up act to another room he always wanted to
play. It was not some glamorous arena or
trendy comedy club. It was just an old studio
in Burbank, and he was used to playing in
front of much larger crowds. So what was the
big deal?

The big deal was that, exactly twenty years
after he first made his bold prediction to Seaholm classmate Pete Shelley, Tim Allen was
finally going to do Carson. He was finally
going to visit America's most famous green
room. Tim was no longer the dirty comic un-
suitable for late-night television. He was the
clean comic who had conquered prime time.

Tim already had a hit series, but in a way
his "Tonight Show" debut, on November 13,
1991, meant that he had finally arrived as a
comedian and, better yet, he had made it
there before his hero retired seven months
later.

As always, Tim was nervous, but as always
he killed. He ran through his standard masculinist repertoire, and the crowd loved it.
"Why are men good at tools?" Tim asked the
audience. "Shop class," he said. "They made
us go to shop class. Why do you listen to shop
teachers? Half of them are missing fingers."

Johnny also loved Tim's act. "That's marvelous stuff," he told him. The king of late-
night television said his stuff was marvelous.

It couldn't get any better than that. Or could it?

You could always tell your position in the industry by how you were treated on "The Tonight Show." Unknowns were squeezed in at the end and could often get bumped if other guests went on too long. More well established performers were guaranteed some time on the sofa, and given a chance to plug their upcoming appearances. Major stars got to go on first and could even leave early.

On his first appearance, Tim got time on the sofa. Tim Allen had status.

It was another night in his life he would never forget, like the night in Detroit when he first took the stage or the night in Akron when he first found his niche.

"One night, early last year, we're sitting around at the bar outside the main stage of the Comedy Castle, and 'The Tonight Show' comes on," recalled Jim McFarlin, a Detroit reporter who covered him for years, and "Tim looks at me and tells me the exact moment, the date, and the show that he made his first appearance."

Also, that Fall, Tim's second cable special, "Tim Allen Rewires America," aired on Showtime. It was the old Tim, the dirty Tim, talking about burping and farting—all the things he could never discuss on his television show.

As "Home Improvement," however, continued to draw millions of new fans, Tim realized he had to change more than his address—he had to change his act. He had a new reputation to protect, a character to uphold. He was as much Tim Taylor as he was Tim Allen. "I remember Tim coming on stage after (the show) hit, and all of a sudden, he looked at the audience, and there were all these kids," recalled Chris Di Petta. "So he had to edit as he went along in his routine. It was funny watching him trying to be funny without saying anything dirty."

He didn't like the new act. "The problem is, so much of my humor is spontaneous," he told *Ladies' Home Journal,* "and you lose that when you have to think, 'I can't do this, can't say that—oops, better not tell that joke.' It doesn't have the same rock 'n' roll feeling that it used to, and I miss that." On occasion, Allen would perform two shows—an early, wholesome performance for the youngsters, and a late, unrestrained show for the adults.

In general, though, Tim adjusted well to his new position in the world. Maybe it was because it came relatively late—he was almost forty. He loved his new life. It was the best life he ever had.

His new life, for instance, gave him the opportunity to test-drive the new Dodge Viper down Sunset Boulevard. Jason Vines, a former Detroit comedian who was doing public relations for Chrysler, called Tim one day to see if he might be interested in taking the car for a spin. Of course, he was interested. This was Tim Allen, the motorhead from the Motor City. Maybe in high school he couldn't drive the best cars down Woodward Avenue because he didn't have a father who worked for the auto industry. But this wasn't high school anymore, and in Hollywood he was near the top of his class.

Maybe so, but Tim sometimes talked like a kid who expected to be expelled at any moment.

On one hand, doing time in prison had been great preparation for show business. If he could deal with the Bubbas in Sandstone, he could certainly deal with the bastards in Hollywood.

On the other hand, his life as Tim Dick made it tough for him to trust his life as Tim Allen. He had lost his father at eleven, and his freedom at twenty-six. How could he be certain his fame wasn't next?

"I'm still kind of a conservative guy," he told the *Los Angeles Times.* "My wife and I are waiting for the bottom to fall out, or the network to decide we're going to go against '60 Minutes.'"

ABC wasn't that daring, although who knows? Maybe Tim might have given Mike Wallace and company a tough battle in the ratings. "Home Improvement" finished the 1991-92 season in fifth place, the only breakout hit on any network. The other shows in the top five—"60 Minutes," "Roseanne," "Murphy Brown," and "Cheers"—were established forces. "Home Improvement" was on its way to becoming one. The show was attracting big support from thirty-five-to-forty-four-year-olds and people making more than $50,000 a year.

In 1992, *Entertainment Weekly* polled readers

to choose the funniest actor on television. Allen, the newcomer, didn't stand a chance against the likes of Bill Cosby, Jerry Seinfeld, and John Goodman. But things change quickly in Hollywood. Tim Allen was the people's choice, the new champion of prime time, the new Cosby. The man with the blemished past suddenly had the brightest future.

"This popularity scares me s——less," he told the magazine in his typical cautiousness. "They're probably building me up so they can tear me down."

21

The public weren't the only ones building him up. Allen, in fact, was so highly regarded by ABC after his rookie season that the network decided to give him another test.

Up until then, he had enjoyed a relatively free ride, positioned perfectly between two heavyweights—"Full House" and "Roseanne." The show had done much better than expected, far outranking "Head of the Class," which had occupied the same lofty spot a year earlier. But it was still far from certain how "Home Improvement" would fare on its own, in a less-enviable time period. ABC was determined to find out.

The test would not be easy. The network wasn't going to pit Tim against some lightweight. Tim was going to face another talent of his stature.

Jerry Seinfeld.

On the surface, it would be a hard-fought duel between the two former stand-ups, but being in the same profession was about all that Tim Allen and Jerry Seinfeld had in common.

Tim represented the comfort of Middle America. Seinfeld stood for the chaos of New York City.

Tim represented the bewildered husband. Seinfeld stood for the bewildered single guy.

Tim was mechanical. Seinfeld was mental.

In any case, the two would stage a pivotal battle for Madison Avenue and the American people. ABC took one look at the demographics and figured that Tim didn't need Roseanne Barr to get good ratings.

The show, in fact, had better numbers than its lead-in, "Full House," which was no small accomplishment. Tim, in just his first season on the air, had finally bypassed his old friend from Detroit, Dave Coulier. Now it was Coulier who had every reason to be jealous.

By moving Tim opposite Seinfeld, the network hoped to establish a potent Wednesday night lineup. If Tim could knock him off, that would surely help the other shows, which included "The Wonder Years" and "Doogie Howser, M.D.," and earn more megabucks for ABC.

But the move posed some risks. Maybe a lot of Tim's success was due to his cushy spot a half hour before the diva of television. Maybe he wasn't ready to take charge of a lineup by himself. Maybe, as he feared, the bottom was about to fall out, after all.

On the other hand, Tim was always ready to embrace a new challenge, and taking on

someone as highly regarded as Jerry Seinfeld
was about as challenging as it could get in
the television business. Even though "Seinfeld" had finished far back in the ratings the
year before, it had captured an Emmy for best
writing in a comedy series, and had been
nominated for eight others. It was the media's
favorite, and it figured to do even better this
time.

One source of concern for Tim and the network was that, by moving the show from 8:30
P.M. to 9:00 P.M., it might become too late for
one of its most cherished constituencies—the
kids. "Home Improvement" had frequently
finished first among children ages 2–11. Many
teenagers were drawn to the show by the
three boys, especially actor Jonathan Taylor-
Thomas, a budding heartthrob.

The later time slot, though, did hold a few
advantages. Tim and his talented writers
could take more latitude to explore adult
themes. Either way, it was the most highly
anticipated network matchup since Fox had
the nerve to pit "The Simpsons" against "The
Cosby Show" in 1990.

For Tim, it was nothing personal. He even
called Seinfeld to apologize. "As stupid as it
was, I just wanted him to know," Tim told
USA Today, "that I had nothing to do with
the decision to move the show. Two comics
are doing pretty damn well, and we have to
be moved right against each other."

Apologetic or not, Tim was going to do his
best to beat his friend. In 1992, he cohosted
the Emmy Awards with Kirstie Alley and

Dennis Miller, a remarkable sign of clout for a comic with only one year of prime-time experience. Always the self-promoter, Tim thought it would be a good way to plug the time change.

The match against "Seinfeld" turned out to be a mismatch. The numbers grew so miserable for NBC that it eventually surrendered, moving "Seinfeld" to Thursday nights, where it became a Top 5 hit. ABC was right. Tim Allen didn't need Roseanne Barr. He could carry his own night of programming.

But, while he may have collected better numbers, he did not collect better notices. Once again, the press gave more favorable coverage to Jerry Seinfeld. They could better identify with a New York bachelor than a Michigan father of three. While "Home Improvement" was focusing on the family, "Seinfeld" was delving into such topics as female nipples exposed on Christmas cards and masturbation. Ironically, during their club circuit days, Tim was known as the dirty comic while Jerry Seinfeld was one of the cleanest.

Over time, Tim started to see himself as the Rodney Dangerfield of the small screen. "It seemed as if we were being ignored simply because we were popular," he later told *USA Today*. "We work as hard as anybody else, and for it always to be inferred that we're not clever because we're a family show seemed unfair."

If Tim didn't get all the respect he deserved, he certainly earned a lot of other rewards. In 1993, he moved into a new house in the San Fernando Valley, a four-bedroom, fifty-five hundred-square-footer with a large backyard and pool. According to *USA Today*, the property was constructed in 1947 by a Hollywood science fiction director, which was only fitting: Tim Allen's career had gone into orbit. He was now in a position to meet the top people in almost any field. Tim, naturally, chose to meet the top people in auto racing, including Steve Saleen, a race car specialist based in Southern California.

One night in early 1993, when Tim was set to play at a comedy club in Hermosa Beach, he made arrangements for Saleen and his crew to bring a few cars around to check out. Tim, the car nut in real life, had made himself Tim Taylor, the car nut, on television. "When we pulled up," Saleen recalled, "he was waiting there at the curb for us. I barely got out of the car before he came over, introduced himself to me, and said, 'Let's go for a ride,' so before he went on his routine, we were cruising around Redondo and Hermosa Beach."

Cruising around wasn't enough for Tim. He made plans with Saleen to work together on a supercharged, six hundred-horsepower, forty thousand dollar 1993 Mustang, or "the ultimate Mustang," as the race car designer calls it. Gerald Dick, the father who passed his love for automobiles on to his son, would have been so proud. "As a kid," Allen told *USA Today*, "I used to go to auto shows and look at prototype cars and wonder what it would be like to build them. Now, some of my dreams are coming true."

Tim didn't forget about the Motor City, either. Even if he was becoming firmly settled in Hollywood, each spring, when "Home Improvement" went on its hiatus, Tim and his family went back to his home in Michigan. For years, he had spent week after week on the road to afford it, and he wasn't going to sell it now. Michigan also served as a much-needed retreat from the demands of the entertainment industry, and as an opportunity for Tim to get reacquainted with his family and old friends.

Tim Allen never rests for long. During the summer after the show's first season, for example, he took off on a thirty-city concert tour, and found time to tape a series of commercials for Builders Square, a chain of home improvement centers. A few months later, he headlined a benefit at the Birmingham Theater to assist Forgotten Harvest, a Michigan group that distributes food to the hungry and homeless. Tim has always given back to the state that has given him so much.

Once back home, Tim was no prima donna. Even if millions tuned in to see him every Wednesday night, he was still the same old Tim, the same class cutup from Seaholm High. No matter how famous he had become, Tim was still terrified before every stand-up performance. During one return visit in late 1993, Tim performed at one of his old hangouts, the Holly Hotel, and seemed as anxious as if it were 1983.

"I was amazed," said George Kutlenios, the hotel owner. "I thought Tim would just be able to walk up there and kind of get it out of the way. But Tim is pacing back and forth like it's his first night on stage, going over material, bouncing stuff off of me. I said, 'You could go out there right now and pick your nose for forty minutes, and these people would love you.' He just wouldn't accept that. He was terrified of flopping. And this is Holly, Michigan, not Sunset Boulevard."

Tim had nothing to worry about. He wasn't going to flop on a stage in Holly, Michigan, and he wasn't going to bomb anywhere else, either. The bottom was not about to fall out. In fact, through a deal which ABC had made with Wind Dancer Productions, the company which produced "Home Improvement," Tim was guaranteed to stay on the air through the 1995-96 season. It was an unprecedented vote of confidence for a show still only in its second season, and an unprecedented vote of confidence for Tim Allen.

Months later, Tim received even more security. Disney began to sell reruns of the show to local stations. Sources were speculating that based on initial sales, "Home Improvement" had the chance to gross well over $2.5 million per episode, and that if the show managed to stay on the air for at least eight years, which was a very good possibility, it could eventually generate more than $600 million in rerun revenue, second only to "The Cosby Show," which earned nearly $900 million in syndication.

Tim was set for life. The comic who had once joked about taking a swan dive off the balcony, who had seriously wondered if he was ever going to make any money with his talent, was making millions.

His talent was also earning him more than monetary rewards. In the fall of 1993, exactly two years after he had taken a seat on the most famous sofa in America and conversed with Johnny for the first time, Tim was asked to speak to another American legend—Barbara Walters. Perhaps even more than an appearance on Carson, an appearance with Walters signified Tim had reached yet another plateau in his career.

True to form, Barbara did not hold back. Both during the introduction and in her questions, she brought up the two biggest tragedies in Tim's past—his dad's death and his drug dealing.

She asked him why he hadn't been in the car that afternoon when the family went to the University of Colorado football game, and if he felt guilty about it. Tim said the decision to hang around the neighborhood with Bobby Click probably saved his life. "I would have sat where I usually sit (next to his dad) and it crushed his side of the car and I would have died. I've replayed that a million times."

Regarding his life in Kalamazoo, Tim said: "In those days, it seemed everybody was selling marijuana. I'm not trying to make it seem any less than it was, 'cause I have more guilt about that than (about) my father. It was a nasty business. It was a wonderful thing to

get caught. If I hadn't gotten caught, I probably would have become very good at that.
I was becoming very good at it. If the drug
conviction hadn't happened, I would have
never straightened my life around." He gave
Laura a lot of credit, as well, for his recovery.
"It was very important to have someone to
hang on to."

Tim also told Barbara about prison, about
the humiliating ordeal of being strip-searched
every time before he went to church, and how
he had used his humor to survive.

Once again, Tim Allen brought Tim Dick
out of hiding, and there was nothing to worry
about. The coast was clear. Tim was a star,
and the past couldn't change a thing.

22

There wasn't much left for Tim Allen to conquer.

First he became one of the best club comics in the Midwest. Then he took his act to Los Angeles and won over Michael Eisner, Jeffrey Katzenberg, and the rest of the Disney empire. From there he got his own television show and won over a whole nation. While his peers didn't give him an Emmy, and the press didn't give him respect, his public more than made up for it. He finished on top of the ratings, and won the People's Choice award as the funniest actor in a television comedy. He had conquered it all.

Well, not exactly. Tim Allen still hadn't taken that other traditional step in the entertainment business.

He hadn't become a movie star.

On the surface, it seemed an unlikely scenario. Sure, the tool man could stay in character week after week as the bumbling, yet well-intentioned, Tim Taylor. His role, frankly, didn't demand too much depth. He was still a comic first, an actor second. As he told Johnny Carson one night: "I'm not really an actor. I just play one on TV." Thus, what proof was there that he possessed the range to make it to the big screen?

Some performers simply belong on television, and nowhere else. They are the perfect size. But, when they try to branch out to become movie stars—i.e. Bill Cosby, Roseanne Barr, Shelley Long, Henry Winkler—they are overwhelmed by the screen. Their personas, for whatever reason, simply can't expand into the wider world of motion pictures. Suddenly they look small, insignificant, almost invisible. There was every reason to believe the same thing would happen to Tim Allen.

Tim, in fact, seemed to be in no hurry to prove otherwise. He was quite content to be a star on television and to keep people laughing with his stand-up routine. He knew his boundaries with the public, and didn't try to cross them. "It wasn't my intent to do a movie," he told the *Los Angeles Daily News*. "I never wanted to be a movie star, none of that (garbage)."

But Disney had other plans for him, and why not? Tim was about as bankable as it gets in Hollywood. Each week, millions watched his television show. Why wouldn't they pay to see him in the theater?

The challenge was coming up with the appropriate project. If he was going to try motion pictures, he was going to have to choose something that utilized his unique talents, and had a chance of success at the box office.

One day, it arrived. The script came from screenwriters Leo Benvenuti and Steve Rudnick, two comedians he knew from Chicago. It was about the most sympathetic character Tim could ever hope to portray—Santa Claus.

Tim read it while on vacation in Palm Springs and immediately fell in love with the whole concept. He showed it to Laura, who had the same reaction. "I had never read a screenplay before," he told the *Times.* "We both cried and laughed."

One day, he casually mentioned his interest to Disney's Jeffrey Katzenberg. The studio bigwig read it, agreed it was the perfect project for his hottest property, and that was that: Tim Allen was going to do a movie. Katzenberg, according to published reports, was so adamant that Tim play Santa that he put the project on hold for an entire year until the star could squeeze the time in his schedule to do it.

At first, however, Outlaw Productions, according to manager Richard Baker, didn't put Tim at the top of their list. "They were hoping to attract actors like Tom Hanks, and a director like Ron Howard," Baker told the *Los Angeles Times.*

But Baker and Messina persisted. They had won over Showtime's Dennis Johnson and the Disney bureaucracy, and now they would persuade Outlaw that Tim, indeed, was the *only* one for the role.

Nonetheless, the move represented a huge

career gamble for Tim. Even if he gave an admirable performance, and the film managed to tap into the comedic qualities that made him a television superstar, there was still no guarantee that the public would shell out seven dollars to see it. A few bad reviews, the wrong word of mouth, and the whole thing could be a flop.

For Tim, the consequences could be serious, perhaps even threatening his invincibility, and proving to the people in power that he didn't, after all, possess the right stuff to make the tough transition to motion pictures. Next time they might not be so willing to bankroll him.

With so much at stake, Tim certainly didn't hesitate to use his influence. He reportedly convinced Disney to hire John Pasquin as director. Pasquin had no experience at the helm of a feature film, but the star had plenty of confidence in him. Pasquin had directed the first season of "Home Improvement."

The shoot took place in Toronto in the spring of 1994, just after Allen had wrapped up his third season on television. Originally, as Allen had pictured it, the film was supposed to have somewhat of a dark, modern edge. Tim's character was going to gun down the real Santa when he caught him breaking into his house.

But Disney, hoping to capture a holiday audience, understood the marketing value of proceeding with a much safer scenario. You can't allow Santa to be shot in front of millions of kids, and expect to make any money out of it. Instead, Pasquin convinced Tim that the movie had to become more of a heart-warming story about the reconciliation between a father and his son.

The story revolved around Scott Calvin (Tim), a divorced workaholic who hadn't spent enough time with his eight-year-old son. Stuck together on Christmas Eve, they hear a noise on their roof. It's Santa, but he's been seriously injured, and must hand his Christmas packages to Calvin. It was the perfect holiday picture for the splintered family of the nineties.

At first, however, Disney didn't make the film one of its top priorities. Even with its most popular property as the lead actor, the studio wasn't in any mood to spend a lot of money on the project. According to *Entertainment Weekly*, it was "shot in a sort of gigantic toolshed ... the relatively pinchpenny budget accommodating an epic North Pole toy factory but not a soundstage.

"It was awful," Rudnick told the magazine. "You'd get tugboats and planes going by (delaying shooting because of noise). The set was hot, kids (who played Santa's 125 elves) were passing out ... That Tim comes across as a jolly guy, knowing how miserable he was—that's acting."

Eventually Disney wised up. Sensing that it might have a potential blockbuster for the holidays, the studio poured another $1 million into more music and special effects, and decided to release the film under the highly regarded Walt Disney Pictures banner instead of the second-rate Hollywood Pictures division.

Tim had a lot of reasons to be in a sour mood on the set. He hadn't been able to get much rest after the series broke for the summer, and he was required to spend hours every day applying uncomfortable makeup so he could look like the real Santa. "It was grueling for him," recalled Kim Flagg, "because this was the hiatus and he didn't get the chance to relax, and was away from Laura and Kady."

The time away from his family had its effect. Once, when Pasquin reminded him of that fact in order to get him to evoke pain in a particularly emotional scene, Allen went nuts. "He's under tremendous pressure," Pasquin told *Entertainment Weekly*. "Disney's trying to get as much out of him as possible."

No doubt about that. Besides the television show and the movie, Disney had, believe it or not, even more plans for Tim Allen. They wanted him to capitalize on the other popular commercial venture for the hot showbiz properties of the nineties.

They wanted him to write a book.

Jerry Seinfeld had done it. Paul Reiser was in the process of doing it. Why couldn't Tim do it? After all, Tim had more viewers than either of them.

Disney, in fact, had first considered the idea a couple of years earlier, but Tim had reportedly told them to wait. He was always good at knowing the right time to market himself. Yet a few years later, even when the timing made more sense, it wasn't easy for Disney to persuade him to finally do it.

"Tim didn't have the time," Dean Valentine said, "and he didn't see the point to doing a book, and if he really wanted to do a book, he really wanted to write it. But from the company's point of view, it was very important for him to do a book. We thought the book would support a show, and the show could support the book, so it was fairly important for us to get him to agree to do a book."

Valentine put Allen in touch with Bob Miller, editor of Hyperion, Disney's book division, and "Tim finally agreed to do one in his spare time."

Disney, Tim told *Entertainment Weekly*, "wanted ... pretty much a yukfest." Seinfeld had written a joke book, and it had become a best-seller. But Tim didn't want to do what Seinfeld did. He had a more ambitious concept in mind.

With the help of writer David Rensin, Tim, from his trailer on the set of *The Santa Clause*, decided to elaborate on some of the central themes of his stand-up act—male-female relationships, masculinism, etc.—and to reveal some deeply personal anecdotes about a past he had kept mostly hidden for many years. The book, entitled, *Don't Stand Too Close to a Naked Man*, was set for a fall release.

Tim did face one major disappointment in 1994. Once again, the Rodney Dangerfield of the sitcoms did not win an Emmy. This time, however, it was not the fault of his peers. It was the fault of his people.

In 1993, he had lost out to Ted Danson, and it was no surprise. Danson was very good, and his long-running hit show, "Cheers," was going off the air. He was the sentimental favorite. A year later, though, with Danson out of the way, Tim stood a much better chance of receiving the award. It would be quite an honor for the ex-comic who needed acting lessons before he taped his first pilot.

Just one problem. His personal staff forgot to submit his name to the Academy of Television Arts and Sciences before the May 11 deadline. Tim wouldn't get a chance to be judged by his fellow actors.

Tim "relies on support people to take care of these kinds of administrative chores," Richard Baker admitted to *People* magazine. "But this time, things just fell through the cracks."

Still, as the summer of 1994 drew to an end, Tim Allen was positioned to accomplish even greater success. The biggest star on television—"Home Improvement" had eclipsed both "Roseanne" and "60 Minutes" to finish the season as the highest-rated show—was about to find out if he could make it as a movie star and author.

23

First, he would have to prove himself on television again.

For the upcoming 1994-95 season, ABC, never content to leave Tim in one time slot for too long, decided it would test his appeal on another night.

Last time, he had been dispatched to duel Jerry Seinfeld, and sent him to another night. This time, the network chose an equally worthy adversary for prime-time warfare.

Kelsey Grammer.

Grammer, of course, had played the well-known psychiatrist from "Cheers," and was reprising the same role in the spinoff "Frasier." The show had been very successful, both commercially and critically, as soon as it hit the airwaves in the Fall of 1993. Like "Seinfeld," it featured another eloquent, fast-talking urbanite.

Last time, ABC shifted Tim to Wednesdays to take over a whole night. This time, the network was trying to stop NBC from doing the same. ABC, showing tremendous respect for him, moved his show into Roseanne's former time slot to challenge "Frasier." The network apparently felt that "Roseanne" was on the decline, but "Home Improvement" was still heading in the opposite direction.

Once again, Tim had mixed feelings about the move, and just as he had done with Seinfeld, he called Grammer to let him know it was nothing personal.

He appreciated the vote of confidence from his superiors, yet he knew there would be a cost. "When ABC switched him from Wednesday back to Tuesday nights," said his stepfather, Bill Bones, "he didn't like it because he knew damn well it was going to affect his ratings. He knew a certain number of people would watch it ('Frasier'), and take away from him."

Or, as Matt Williams told the *Los Angeles Times:* "It's highly unlikely that we're going to be No. 1 again. How much the audience is divided will determine where we fall in the Top 5."

For Tim Allen, always waiting for failure, any decline in the Nielsens, however miniscule and understandable, would only confirm his worst fears, that perhaps his fame was beginning, at last, to bottom out. Perhaps he would be back on the club circuit in no time.

In fact, ever since "Home Improvement" had scaled to the top of the charts, Allen began, according to some, to be almost obsessed with the weekly numbers. He was intensely competitive, and knew there was only one way he could go—down. "Tim wants the show to be Number 1," Ted Harbert, president of ABC Entertainment, told the *New York Times*. "That's just rare in television. Others in television over the decades have taken the opportunity to go Mr. Hollywood."

On one occasion, Harbert said, he showed Tim that the ratings from the night before drew an outstanding 30 share, yet the star was far from satisifed. "He likes to hear me say we had a 33 share," Harbert told the newspaper.

He was even harder on himself, which was nothing new. George Kutlenios, who saw Tim do stand-up numerous times, was constantly amazed at how he perceived himself. "He was always his own worst critic," Kutlenios said. "I'd sit in the back of the room and think some of his new stuff was absolutely terrific. He'd get off the stage and think it was the worst stuff he ever did." Added Allen's good friend Ken Calvert: "Tim is still the guy who says, 'I fucked up that one line.' You say, 'Which line?' And he says, 'Oh, you wouldn't have even noticed it.' "

The self-critical pattern didn't change when he became a big star. During the winter, Jerry Elliott, his former colleague from the early stand-up days in Detroit, visited Tim in Los Angeles. "We watched, oddly enough, 'Home Improvement,' and he second-guesses a lot of his lines or his movements. I was amazed."

As he prepared to face Kelsey Grammer, once again, the press was on the opposite side. " 'Frasier' seems much the wiser, wittier, wackier show," wrote Tom Shales of the *Washington Post*, "a sterling silver sitcom in the best traditions of the genre ... 'Frasier' vs. 'Home Improvement' is ... a matchup between a truly inspired show and a mere proficient piece of craftmanship." "Frasier," incidentally, had won an Emmy the year before as the best comedy series.

Tim had to combat the growing perception among some critics that his show was, as he told the *Los Angeles Times*, "some 600-pound gorilla with no taste that's knocking off these wonderful, eclectic shows."

The truth, however, is that the media has a tendency to create polar opposites to heighten the drama of any showdown, and in this case "Home Improvement" had consistently appealed to a wider cross section of the populace than critics might be willing to admit. One look at the ratings proved it wasn't merely a show for the heartland.

It didn't have to be hip or topical to win over audiences. It didn't have to bring up on-the-edge issues such as masturbation or lesbianism or any other isms. It didn't have to find its way into a Dan Quayle speech or a national debate. All it had to do, and it did it quite efficiently week after week, was bring wholesome entertainment into people's living rooms. The Taylors had become America's new favorite family. As *Gentlemen's Quarterly* put it: "The turf is too familiar to elicit oohs and aahs—just a soft knowing chorus of uh-huhs."

That chorus carried Tim Allen to victory

again in the battle against "Frasier." The first episode of "Home Improvement" was seen in about 21.6 million homes—4 percent higher than its average the year before—compared to 13.8 million for "Frasier." Week after week, the numbers maintained the same general pattern.

Tim Allen was two for two against the best NBC had to offer. He was the undisputed king of prime-time television, and there was no evidence anyone else was going to dethrone him. But Tim Allen won't remember the fall of 1994 for his triumph over Kelsey Grammer. The fall of 1994 will go down as the fall when Tim Allen became a movie star.

In November, *The Santa Clause* made its premiere at the Fox Theatre in Detroit. Tim, never one to forget his roots, made sure Michigan hosted another important event in his career. Kalamazoo, the college town where he almost lost everything, had welcomed him for his breakthrough special on Showtime four years earlier. This time, as Allen had insisted, the scene would be just a few miles away from where he grew up in Birmingham. The local hero was home.

The local hero was also humbled. "Never in my wildest imagination did I believe I'd be standing here like this one day," he told the 3,750 people who packed the theater.

His parents and grandmother showed up at the premiere, and so did many of his old friends. But Tim Allen was a product now as much as a person, and to promote the film, he had to be shuttled from one interview to another. He belonged to a nation now.

Two days later, the film opened across the country. Tim was no longer on familiar ground. He wouldn't be facing competition like Jerry Seinfeld and Kelsey Grammer, who represented great challenges and were outstanding talents but worked in his own environment. They enjoyed large and loyal television followings, as did Tim.

This time, however, he would be going against Tom Cruise and Brad Pitt, two sexy heartthrobs from another generation. Tim had become an outsider trying to break into a very exclusive club, and movie fans don't give out memberships that easily.

In this case, they made an exception. On its first weekend, *The Santa Clause* took home an estimated $19.3 million, becoming Disney's biggest-ever live-action opener, and third-best debut behind *The Lion King* and *Dick Tracy*. Overall, the film finished second in the nation behind Cruise's *Interview With a Vampire*.

Within a few weeks, the film, which cost a relatively paltry $18 million to make, had jumped to number one, and it didn't just rent the spot. It stayed on top week after week, grossing well over $100 million by the end of the year. *The Santa Clause* was clearly the surprise hit of the holiday season.

Then again, how much of a surprise was it? From the start, Tim and his management team had choreographed every single element. They had chosen the right vehicle for his film debut, the right director, the right character, and the right timing. They had brilliantly capitalized on Tim's natural charm and likability. They had done everything they could, and the public had done the rest.

"He chose a comedy, a light comedy," Dean Valentine said. "He chose something very commercial." In one scene, Tim's fictional character picked up a tool belt, an obvious link to his other fictional character, Tim Taylor.

Tim's career would never be the same again. He had proved himself where it mattered the most in Hollywood—at the box office—and if he could do it once, the business was surely going to give him another chance.

Some insiders, according to published reports, immediately speculated that Allen had catapulted himself into the highest echelon of film salaries—between $8 million and $10 million—alongside such established box office superstars as Robin Williams and Tom Hanks. Coupled with his earnings from "Home Improvement"—a reported $5 million a season, or about $200,000 per episode, which includes advances from syndication proceeds—Tim Allen had become one of the richest performers in Hollywood.

Tim was delighted by the movie's success. In many ways, he was still the child who couldn't believe he was faring so well in the adult world. At one screening of the movie in Westwood, recalled Kim Flagg, "He was so cute, just so excited. He was just like a kid watching a movie, grinning and giggling."

The movie was more than just a financial

triumph. He was also given credit for his acting skills. "Although aided by Hollywood
wizardry, Allen makes that transformation (to
Santa) come from within; his is a fine, wide-
ranging portrayal of a man awakening to his
emotions," according to the *Los Angeles Times*.

The praise may actually have meant more
to him than the profit. Here was the comic
who had openly admitted his only experience
was in the background of a Mr. Goodwrench
commercial. Some of the comics who knew
him better than anyone said that Tim Allen
might be funny, but he was no actor. Some
of the Detroit comics were wrong.

24

The fall of 1994 will also be remembered for another milestone in Tim Allen's career.

The book that he had written in his spare time on the set of *The Santa Clause* hit the shelves in late September. Hyperion had high enough expectations to order a first printing of 600,000 copies, a staggering amount for a forty-one-year-old stand-up comic who was still a relative newcomer to celebrity status. He received a reported 1.6-million-dollar advance.

Hyperion, it turned out, had good reason to hype it up. Within a few weeks, *Don't Stand Too Close to a Naked Man,* stood right at the top of the *New York Times* best-seller list. It was a fitting accomplishment for the ex-con who reportedly had passed his time in the joint by devouring any biography he could find. Now he was the one who had written a book.

To be sure, it was no literary masterpiece—

Publishers Weekly, for instance, referred to it as a "strange amalgam of the callow and the sophisticated and the result is only intermittently funny, and then only mildly so." But Tim didn't write the book for a snobby New York publishing magazine. He wrote it for his fans, and they loved it.

The book wasn't purely a collection of jokes, or a philosophy dissertation, or a probing account of his past. It was a combination of all three elements, and that's what made it work—a "remarkably reader-friendly musing, which is at once funny, elliptical, elegant, and mildly philosophical," according to the *Detroit News*.

Much of the book deals with Tim's favorite topic—male-female relationships. He repeated the same message he had conveyed during his stand-up days and on "Home Improvement," that men and women are, essentially, a "different species," who must overcome a lot of fundamental obstacles to find any common ground.

He also took time to write about something he had rarely explored anywhere—his life in prison. It had briefly been part of his stand-up routine, but with his classy wardrobe and disarming looks audiences had trouble picturing him as a hardened criminal. He was also uncomfortable with delving into such a painful chapter of his life.

Then, in 1991, when he had no other choice, he made his clever confession in *USA Today*, providing a few broad, obligatory observations about the lessons he learned from incarceration. He talked about how it had turned his life around, and how he just wanted to get on with his future. The press let him. The story of Tim Allen the drug dealer was dead.

But in his book, for the first time, Tim went much further. He described in detail a few encounters with the characters he confronted behind bars and the strategies he needed to stay alive. He no longer treated prison as a shameful part of his life that he was desperate to shield from his public. Instead, by being vulnerable, with humor and honesty he showed how he had learned to accept his past. This was his ultimate liberation.

He also revealed his real name for the first time, and how much it framed his entire life. It was Tim Dick who created Tim Allen. It was the ridiculed boy who turned into the resilient man. "In retrospect," he wrote, "it made me a better person. Now I have to thank my name for making my life special."

Finally, he wrote about something more traumatic than either his name or his crime— his father's death. That, too, for the longest time, was a subject Tim preferred to avoid, both onstage and in person. Gerald Dick's abrupt departure had, on one afternoon, changed his life forever. The idyllic days of growing up in Denver were replaced by years of anger and pain.

"I realized there is no one here to protect us," he wrote, "that life can be taken from us at any time ... I don't think I took the time to grieve until much later in life, when I suddenly realized how much I missed the guy. I

218   **Michael Arkush**

would like to have known him now that I'm a man.''

The book was a great experience for Tim. Although writing it while working on his first film "seemed absolutely the dumbest thing I'd ever done," he told *Entertainment Weekly*, "I got very introspective with the book ... I came back with a renewed sense of where I'm coming from. It helped me blow out my motors and defoul my spark plugs.''

25

One question about Tim Allen remained: How would he handle any setbacks? It had been a long time since he had a chance to find out. Perhaps, he was disappointed at not winning an Emmy, and maybe even more upset when he didn't get an opportunity a year later. But how would he react if his position in the ratings started to slip?

In 1995, he found out. Ever since ABC had moved his show back to Tuesday nights to challenge "Frasier," Tim had feared that it would push him out of the number one spot. Kelsey Grammer was a pretty potent figure, bound to draw enough viewers away from "Home Improvement" to make a difference, and that's exactly what happened. For the first time in many months, Tim Allen was no longer king of the sitcom, and he didn't take it very well.

"We're in a skirmish, where no one else appears to be in a skirmish," he complained to the media. "Jerry (Seinfeld) and his crew don't have any competition. Roseanne has very little competition. So we're battling this out, and it tends to put a little stress on all of us." And, as he told *Time* magazine: "Frasier is killing us. He's taking away our heat."

He may have fallen slightly in the ratings—to number three by the end of the season—but it didn't do a thing to hurt his reputation. He was one of the few performers, in fact, rumored to be in line to host the 1995 Academy Awards broadcast, an honor only afforded to the elite in Hollywood. It was just as well that he didn't get the chance. He wasn't too excited about the prospect of saying the wrong thing and bombing in front of a few hundred million people.

He also began to explore other careers. In March, he announced, along with race car driver Steve Saleen, the formation of Saleen-Allen RRR Racing. Tim even plans to do some of the racing himself.

As a boy he would go with his father to watch the drag-racing and learn about what makes each car go so fast.

As an adolescent he'd hang out with the gang at Woodward, though he was unable to match his peers, who had more power.

And now as an adult he is the one with the resources to create his own racing team. Maybe he'll even be the next Paul Newman.

Speaking of clout, in the spring of 1995, *TV Guide* made official what many in the industry already suspected:

Tim Allen was the most powerful star in television.

The magazine referred to his triple play of success—the movie, the series, the book—and to the vast revenue anticipated for the show's future syndication. He was, however, no Roseanne. "He's not the kind of guy who would say, 'Let's dump this person or get rid of that person,'" said "Home Improvement" director Andy Cadiff.

He was no pushover, either. He knew how to get what he wanted, whether it had to do with the television series, the movie, the book, or anything else. *TV Guide* pointed out that when Allen mentioned to others that "Home Improvement" didn't have its name on the soundstage, the oversight was quickly corrected, and when Allen brought up the fact that "Tool Time" girl Debbie Dunning wasn't a regular on the show, that was rectified as well.

Why shouldn't he use his tremendous clout? In Hollywood, you may not have it for long. The same people who would drop everything for you in January may not return your phone calls in February. His father had been taken from him when Tim was eleven, and he knew his fame could be just as fleeting.

"It's intoxicating," Allen said in a 1994 interview with the *Los Angeles Times*, referring to his prominence. "To get this much attention, for God's sake, it's intoxicating. When it goes away, there's a little vacuum—I'm not sure what it is."

Tim won't have to worry about finding himself in a vacuum any time soon. He's got plenty more ideas to explore on "Home Improvement," and it's not likely the show will slip much further in the ratings. It may never be on top again, but its wholesome portrayal of family life, complete with the standard husband-wife problems, offers the kind of universal appeal that transcends the traditional fickleness of the television viewer. "This show celebrates and represents the majority of us who love their family, do their best, pay their taxes, and obey the law," Tim told the *Los Angeles Times* in the spring of 1994.

Furthermore, with the show headed for syndication, Tim Allen may be a fixture well into the twenty-first century.

Expect him also on the silver screen. Though he says he's opposed to doing a sequel to *The Santa Clause*, nothing is permanent in Hollywood—Tim will surely be offered other scripts and has reportedly written a science fiction script that, considering his enormous power, might get made. He has also mentioned the possibility of him taking a noncomedic supporting part in an ensemble drama to see if America would accept him as a serious actor. Stay tuned.

It's a tough decision for Tim and his managers: Do they keep recycling variations of his Tim Taylor television persona, taking the risk that audiences might grow tired of the same character? Or do they try to explore opportunities that could show off his versatility as an actor and performer, and thereby pick up new audiences? "It's something that we belabor every day," Richard Baker told the *Wall Street Journal*.

Expect him back on the road, as well. Ever since that winter evening in 1979, when he changed his life by taking the stage at Mark Ridley's Comedy Castle, Tim has been addicted to the applause that can only be generated in live performances. As he started to play bigger auditoriums, the feeling became even more intoxicating. "He told me how the laughter from the back rows came up to him like waves in an ocean," George Kutlenios said. "It overwhelms him."

Above all else, expect him on the small screen. Despite the draw of other creative opportunities in his career, Tim has made it clear that his number one professional commitment remains "Home Improvement." No wonder. It is Tim Taylor, the tool man, who made him rich and famous in the first place. Sure, Matt Williams and the rest of the Disney and ABC crews made the character come alive. But it was Tim Allen, and nobody else, who created the tool man on a desperate night in Akron, Ohio, and it won't be easy to let him go.

Someday, he will, though, and he'll be ready for it. He may even be looking forward to it. Back in 1992, when Tim was in just his second season on "Home Improvement," he told *Ladies' Home Journal* that the concept of six or seven more years of doing the show is "like thinking about marathon running—it makes me hurt in sensitive places."

In any case, Tim won't need a television critic or a network executive to tell him that

America has had enough of the tool man.
He'll know when it's the right time to bow
out. He's always had perfect timing.

By then, perhaps he'll have earned more
than just great ratings. Perhaps he'll have an
Emmy. After last year's screwup, there was
no way Tim's name would be left off the ballot again. Disney's Dean Valentine, in fact,
along with Debbie Dunning, rode in Tim's
"Home Improvement" hot rod to the steps of
the Academy of Television Arts and Sciences
to officially present the nominating ballot.

It was the kind of star treatment that Tim
Allen has earned in Hollywood.

This is one success story that nobody had
to make up.

Epilogue

The most remarkable thing about Tim
Allen is not the fact that he is the most powerful star on television, or that he pulled off
record-setting accomplishments in his first
film and his first book, both in the same year.

The most remarkable thing about Tim Allen
is the hardships he had to overcome to make
a career.

In 1979, his career was kaput. He had made
a big mistake, and because of Michigan's
strict antidrug laws, it looked like he might
have to spend the rest of his life in prison
paying for it. The class cutup was about to
become the class convict, and that would be
it. Game, set, career.

But Tim turned state's evidence and turned
his life around. He did his time and then
never wasted his time again. He found his
gift, developed it, and never took it for
granted. He took responsibility for his past,
and began to take charge of his future. He

225

never forgot where he came from, and he
never lost sight of where he wanted to go.

He was fortunate to have a stepfather who
turned into a father, friends who turned into
a family, and a girlfriend who turned into a
goddess.

Ultimately, though, it was Tim, and nobody
else who changed his life. As Judge McCauley
had told him, Tim had two choices, and he
made the right one.

He could have allowed prison to turn him
into a bitter man, angry at the society that
robbed him of his father and his freedom. Instead, though, prison turned him into a better
man, who was determined to show that he
was not a loser. Going to prison was the
worst thing that ever happened to him—and
the best thing that ever happened to him.

But what is it about his internal makeup
that enabled him to overcome the ordeal of
incarceration and actually use it to his advantage? Why did he survive where so many others had surrendered?

Family and friends surely played an important role, but Tim Dick survived because
he had plenty of practice. Early on, he had
learned how to use humor as his most reliable
ally, both to defend himself from the insensitive peers who made fun of his last name, and
to protect himself from the repressed anger
and pain caused by his father's death. For
many years Tim, as he told Barbara Walters
in 1993: "You end up being mad at first at
nameless people, then you're mad at God for
the longest time, and then just mad."

Tim was crying out for help, which may explain why he turned to drugs and why he got caught.

He wanted someone to rescue him from a lifestyle he could not control. It was as if, only by subjecting himself to the worst possible predicament, behind bars with no place to hide, he could finally begin the long road to his recovery. It worked.

But a man does not spend more than a year in prison without it affecting him for the rest of his life. For years Tim tried to bury his past, lying, if necessary, to keep it out of the newspapers. He was smart enough to understand that if the truth did come out, it could become a label—the convict who became a comic—that would follow him forever.

But in his book he brought his life in prison out into the open. He didn't have to do it. He could have kept on being Tim Allen and left it at that. His fans couldn't have cared less about Tim Dick. But Tim, as he approached middle age, felt it was time to make peace with his past and himself, and he seems much happier for it. "I'm Tim Dick," he told the *Detroit Free Press* earlier this year. "And Tim Dick created all this. Tim Dick runs the show here, and he's still kind of pissed that he had zits and didn't get dates when he wanted them."

What about the other major traumatic experience of his life? How is Tim still affected by his father's death?

For one thing, it has taught him to take nothing for granted. He often seems to be waiting for the worst. "It's the soap opera story," he told the *Free Press*. "As soon as someone says, 'I've never loved you more than I love you right now,' boom, he's got a stroke. I think throat cancer, death, something's going to happen." Added former writer partner Eric Head: "Tim could be walking off the stage with an Emmy, and he would say, 'Gosh, I think they got this wrong, I don't know. I don't want to tell anyone just yet. . . . He's always looking over his shoulder."

At last, however, with his amazing accomplishments in recent years—the movie, the book, the television show, the syndication deal, etc.—Tim has grown to trust his own success. It is not some mirage. The bottom is not about to fall out. He is not about to get throat cancer.

Today, thirty-one years after his father's accident, Tim has come full circle. He is forty-two, the exact same age Gerald Dick was when he died. He is now the father. He is now the one who must protect the child. He is very strict about making sure his daughter, Kady, stays out of the spotlight, that she grows up as normal as possible for the child of a Hollywood celebrity. He wants to give her the idyllic upbringing that tragedy forced him to give up.

Tim is also still trying to protect the child in himself. "Underneath the image," Tim told the *Detroit News*, "there's a 14-year-old boy that needs to be protected, so I've developed this 'guy' that protects this 14-year-old boy."

But will Tim Allen ever be completely satisfied? Perhaps not.

"With Tim's makeup, with where he's been," said one friend, "no matter what, it's not going to be enough for him. In the back of his mind, he still has something else to prove to somebody."

So far, Tim Allen has proved quite a bit.

MICHAEL ARKUSH, a staff writer for the *Los Angeles Times*, lives with his wife, Pauletta Walsh, and daughter, Jade, in Pacific Palisades, California. Arkush wrote *Rush!*, a biography of Rush Limbaugh, and co-wrote *60 Years of USC-UCLA Football*.

The Best in Biographies from Avon Books

IT'S ALWAYS SOMETHING
by Gilda Radner   71072-2/ $5.95 US/ $6.95 Can

RUSH!
by Michael Arkush   77539-5/ $4.99 US/ $5.99 Can

STILL TALKING
by Joan Rivers   71992-4/ $5.99 US/ $6.99 Can

I, TINA *by Tina Turner and Kurt Loder*
                             70097-2/ $5.99 US/ $7.99 Can

ONE MORE TIME
by Carol Burnett   70449-8/ $4.95 US/ $5.95 Can

PATTY HEARST: HER OWN STORY
by Patricia Campbell Hearst with Alvin Moscow
                             70651-2/ $5.99 US/ $6.99 Can

SPIKE LEE
by Alex Patterson   76994-8/ $4.99 US/ $5.99 Can

**OBSESSION: THE LIVES AND TIMES OF
CALVIN KLEIN**
by Steven Gaines and Sharon Churcher
                             72500-2/$5.99 US/$7.99 Can